SACRED CURIOSITY

SACRED CURIOSITY

WONDERING OUR WAY TOWARD WHOLENESS

BRITNEY WINN LEE

Broadleaf Books
Minneapolis

SACRED CURIOSITY
Wondering Our Way Toward Wholeness

30 29 28 27 26 25 1 2 3 4 5 6 7 8 9

Library of Congress Cataloging-in-Publication Data

Names: Lee, Britney Winn author
Title: Sacred curiosity : wondering our way toward wholeness / Britney Winn Lee.
Description: Minneapolis : Broadleaf Books, [2026]
Identifiers: LCCN 2025022914 (print) | LCCN 2025022915 (ebook) | ISBN 9798889834694 paperback | ISBN 9798889834700 ebook
Subjects: LCSH: Curiosity
Classification: LCC BF323.C8 L44 2026 (print) | LCC BF323.C8 (ebook) | DDC 248.8/6--dc23/eng/20250916
LC record available at https://lccn.loc.gov/2025022914
LC ebook record available at https://lccn.loc.gov/2025022915

Cover image: © Getty Images / Moments Colllection; Firefly Wonderland by Chakarin Wattanamongkol
Cover design: Amanda Kain

Print ISBN: 979-8-8898-3469-4
eBook ISBN: 979-8-8898-3470-0

For the babies that would have been,
whose breadcrumbs we kept following.

Contents

Contents

Introduction

Outside, the summer air felt soupy and unstable, with the possibility of storms. Inside, clutching a rust-colored throw pillow and tissues, I watched heavy-bottomed raindrops begin to thud onto dirty pebbles and wondered why I had not been collected enough to remember an umbrella. My counselor sat across from me in the antique light of a small lamp, rubbing her hands together like a thoughtful praying mantis. She took her time to respond.

The year's burdens had been building, and it seemed that all of the "boundary work" we'd been needling away at diligently in her office every two weeks was doing little more than keeping me alive. Which wasn't nothing. Five failed rounds of fertility treatments had left me with a concussion from drug-induced dizziness, mounting medical bills, and a depleted spirit. I'd recently served on the jury for a horrific double-murder trial that shook my faith in human goodness, preached a child's funeral for the first time, and watched my dear friend navigate the sudden loss of her mother. At work, a toxic environment was grinding me down, while online, my recently published children's book was drawing hate mail from people who hadn't read it. My denomination was undergoing a split, war footage filled every screen, and beneath it all ran the steady current of everyday stresses: pandemic aftermath, parenting worries, empty gas tanks, and piled dishes. That week, crossing the bridge to another meeting, I'd thought, "If I just turned into the water, I wouldn't have to go to work." I didn't want to be harmed, or gone; I just didn't want to spend another second gulping for breath between blows.

"We've been working for months on defensive approaches like drawing boundaries and practicing mindfulness," I quietly uttered. "But are there any offensive tools you can offer me? Everything feels like it's dead or dying, corroding or corrupted. It feels like I'm not seeing color, and I can't remember what it was like for life not to be gray."

She wasn't alarmed. It's always a gift when someone can offer their unruffled reactions to your humanity. She showed no concern, no shock or emergency. She simply looked up, then down, then rubbed her hands together and pondered as I watched the rain, safe in a moment of unrushed vulnerability.

"I've been reading a book about awe," she eventually said, as if I'd asked for a library recommendation and not just exposed my darkest ruminations. "I think you might like it. There is much in there about how we, in our great loss, grief, and stuckness, can discover renewal in awe and wonder. I have a feeling you may find color again in curiosity—that ever-approachable door to the things that take our breath away and remind us why life is worth it."

She had not suggested that I must labor painstakingly, unsustainably to find the beginnings of relief. She had also not offered me arrival. Rather, she had given me a breadcrumb. It turned out to be enough for the day.

I've been turning that breadcrumb over and over in my mind ever since. There was something profound in the suggestion that curiosity—this most accessible of human capacities hidden in plain sight—might be a pathway back to color, back to life. To put more churchy language to it, you could say that I've been toying with the idea of curiosity as a means of grace. As the old hymn says, "Come thou fount of every blessing, tune my heart to sing Thy grace." Shortly following what would turn out to be this critical therapy session, I got a bee in my bonnet that curiosity may help with the tuning. I haven't been able to let it go.

So, this is a book about curiosity. It's also a book about grace and resurrection. It's a record of my exploration into, and musing on, how curiosity might be one of our most approachable and transformative resources in a world that often feels overwhelming. When everything seems to be burning down around us—from our institutions to our certainties to our connections—curiosity offers an unexpected pathway back to color, back to life.

In my lived experience, research, and writing, I've found curiosity to be a precious and timely tool for lessening the violence, shame, overwhelm, and isolation of our world and adding to its deeply needed awe, connection, creativity, and hope. I hated and feared less at the end of this journey; what a joy it would be if you could say the same.

What have I found in exploring curiosity that I want to tell you beforehand?

That curiosity is bottomless by nature, and so this book is anything but exhaustive.

That curiosity can be approached curiously—through angles, layers, and breadcrumbs. If nothing else, may it give you a starting place to run with.

That I have experienced curiosity as a gift and a posture, a grace and a practice, a lens and a muscle. My confidence in it as vital for those of us here, now, at this point in history has grown exponentially.

That I hope, maybe most of all, that you'll leave these pages holding curiosity as an indispensable value for transformation rather than a limited luxury or trait.

That you'll have held space for how one more question, one more consideration, one more lingering pause or vulnerable opening could be the bridge that moves enemy to friend, hopelessness to healing, and shame to liberation. As Dr. Amy G. Oden says, "Curiosity is a fundamental Christian practice."

There are many ways to engage with this book, and I'll offer some suggestions, but mostly I hope you'll navigate it in whatever setting, company, and pace allows your own curiosity to play most freely and fully. In addition to this introduction, there are twelve chapters followed by four reflection prompts each. We designed it this way so that you and/or a small group of people could break it up evenly over four weeks, six weeks, twelve weeks, or just as many months. The reflection prompts are written to work for communal discussion or personal meditation and journaling. For extra insight, chapter 11 holds a good number of Christmas references and therefore, the book could be used during the season of Advent to supplement a *curious* Christmas.

I should say I'm no theological specialist nor scientific researcher in the field of curiosity, though I do mix quite a bit of the two with personal stories and a few rabbit-trail ramblings throughout the book. Rather, I am an author, seminarian, and nonprofit professional trying to use writing to make more room, as others have so graciously made room for my continually evolving self over the years. The journey from the worship of certainty to the growing freedom and healing of curiosity hasn't been linear. I am forever learning about my own privilege, limitations, and compulsions, cyclically, it seems. I have eaten my words and made a lot of mistakes, mimicked fearful leaders, and added to the brokenness. I've been shown mercy; I try to write from its lessons. Everything I create now—from sermons to essays to captions—flows from my experience of needing people I never thought I'd need. This has awakened me to all that might exist beyond our current constructs, languages, assumptions, boundaries, and presumed endings. That gives me hope. Mostly, I feel like a hound hunting for grace's third way, following those breadcrumbs of curiosity wherever they might lead. I hold to the idea that, as my friend Katelyn says, "God can't only be found in being correct."

Maybe—and this is the whole point—God (and healing, and well-being, and wholeness, and grace, and resurrection) can also and exponentially be found in being curious.

"Prone to wonder, Lord I feel it." May we all be increasingly so.

One

Curiosity Is Accessible

Give us today our daily bread.

(Matthew 6:11)

"This is not the end."

These are the dark orange letters stenciled on top of the whitewashed acrylic painting in my living room, which I look at every morning and every evening.

Its invitation to the observer? Not to assume arrival, but instead, to be reminded that there is so often something else to learn past judgments, somewhere else to go past the bottom, someone else to become past broken, some other lens through which to consider past division, some piece of the story not yet seen, some layer of the person not yet witnessed. Its five words are resurrective in nature, smacking of freedom from oppression, homecoming for exiles, empty tombs for executions, and morning mercies for hard nights—the sort of impossible arcs that we know in our bones are unlikely but for God through love. But it's easy to stick words like *freedom/oppression* and *homecoming/exiles* in close proximity in books like these. Meanwhile, any person being halfway honest knows what chasms can exist between realities in real life. We need bridges to help us over. When I read these orange words, they remind me that curiosity (and its grace) may just be a graspable way to build them.

I need this reminder because it's hard to be human.

Readers who have wondered whether the world we live in has advanced technologically and sociopolitically more quickly than our brains and bodies have been able to evolve are not alone. Sure, there are evidence-backed claims to suggest that in the long view of history, humanity is and has been trending toward betterment and a more peaceful existence. And those are nothing to sneeze at; good news through good data is a gift.

However, you'd be hard-pressed, I believe, to convince our peripheral nervous systems of such findings. While we may, all things considered, be a more peaceful people than we've ever been (this is painful science to hold while bombs explode in the Middle East), we are also more globally connected than ever before thanks to advanced travel and the internet—specifically social media and entertainment news. This means we are shouldering unprecedented amounts of pressure through a constant infiltration of knowledge, expectations, and judgments for which generations before had no experience, let alone strategy. While my great-grandmother would have fielded updates from little more than the gossip, pulpit, and papers of her 230-person town ninety years ago, I could give you gut-wrenching and stressful updates from twelve different loose connections I have in three different countries and multiple states just this week.

"In a modern world, filled with distractions that our ancestors never had the detriment to deal with and that we did not have an opportunity to evolve intuitive mechanisms for," Alexander Kourt, author of *The Curiosity Gene*, writes, "levels of depression and anxiety are far higher than a hundred years ago despite life being far more comfortable than ever." Collective overwhelm and burnout would be enough of a jungle to navigate independently. Joined, though, with the massive isolation of Western society, which is my context, and which convinces us that said burnout is individual and not communal or institutional, and it all feels like an impossibly large pill to swallow. *How do we get better in all of this too-muchness?*

Recent findings suggest that curiosity may just be the highly accessible, ever-present onramp to another way of being human that we desperately need in these times. In one study about the relationship between curiosity and emotional exhaustion for college students, researchers found that students who more often practiced the simple pursuit of novel experiences, knowledge, and meaning in their mundane lives demonstrated more resilience to bounce back from emotional exhaustion. Relatedly, conversations continue to build in recovery and ADHD communities attesting to curiosity's power to assist those with neurodivergent or addicted minds in shifting their "nervous systems from fight-or-flight to rest-and-digest."

When we are in the thick of burnout, overwhelm, or loss, it can seem counterintuitive to "add" or "pursue" anything—I've known these feelings intimately. Surely, we must *check out* for a while before we can ever imagine *tuning in*. I can remember when my son was fresh and soft and new in this world, and we were learning the sleep hacks of first-time parents. I had been processing aloud, and to no one in particular, about needing to keep our baby awake so that he would sleep later or longer when a seasoned dad friend of ours mentioned kindly that "sleep begets sleep." What he meant, I learned, was that an overtired four-month-old would be less likely to fall asleep than one who had gotten a good nap, thus perpetuating our restless nights.

I thought about this on a walk around the neighborhood recently as that once-four-month-old-now-fourth-grader talked my ear off about his latest Minecraft creation, as I dragged our undersocialized dogs away from barking at every neighbor who passed and slugged along with too little sleep and too much scheduled for the week. While his voice and their howls faded to muffled tones momentarily, I thought about the possibility of curiosity as burnout's accessible antidote and fantasized about how I would rather be curled into a recliner watching mindless television and napping for a week than mindfully consider one more novel or meaningful thing. Still, I wondered if, like daily bread, curiosity wouldn't require more of me than I felt I had to give. It seemed to be asking only that I take one small bite, ask one small question, notice one small detail to somehow, like loaves multiplying, allow a meager moment of wonder to sustain me. I decided to experiment with the latter.

"Can we sit for a second?" I asked my kid as we pulled up to a hunter-green park bench, and our pups, worn out from protecting us from nothing, curled under its shade. "Look at that fountain gushing," I noted of the water in front of us, interrupting his almost-launch into another digital world description. "What if that were the spout of a whale that no one knew was living in the bayou?"

"Yeah!" he said, eventually, catching on, "and what if all those ripples were actually faces of naiads like in the Percy Jackson books?" In the distance, a woodpecker *thonk-thonked* on a cypress trunk as I asked, "And what if that sound was the sound of tiny gnomes building a city underground?" "And what if," he mused as a dragonfly bobbed past, "that's Roger, the one I saved with the broken wing on my trampoline last week? Hi, Roger! Are you Roger?!"

We both fell quiet and breathed. Then, staggered by just a few seconds and to our great surprise, a majestic blue crane lit on a branch to our right, bending it like a seesaw, as a mama duck weaved in and out of green algae to our left, leading a trail of eight fuzzy brown babes. We gasped, mouths agape, eyes wide.

Each tiny observation felt like breaking bread together. None alone was a meal, but together, we were fed back to vibrancy. I returned home filled and no longer in need of mindless recuperation. Tuning in had afforded me more than checking out possibly could have, though the math didn't seem logical. Curiosity begot curiosity, life begot life.

"We can find awe anywhere," Dacher Keltner, author and co-director of the Greater Good Science Center writes. "Because doing so doesn't require money or the burning of fossil fuels—or even much time. Our research suggests that just a couple of minutes a day will do. Because we have a basic need for awe wired into our brains and bodies, finding awe is easy if we just take a moment and wonder."

***

The accessibility of curiosity may offer not only relief to inundated individuals but also to whole systems and bodies who have, for so long, adopted and perpetuated the pressures of certainty and *right-knowing*.

Instead of sitting across another table for another meeting, Pastor Betsy asked me to walk through the church's adjacent woods with her as we discussed the upcoming happenings in the life of the congregation. I was set to step into an associate local pastor appointment following her upcoming retirement as the church's senior clergy. She was offering me an incremental master class in approaching church leadership with palms wide open.

"This bike path was made by a father and son during lockdown," she pointed to the thin trail we were following. "And this is where we held a contemplative prayer service under the tree canopy." As we approached the back of the property, a creek gurgle grew louder as gray rocks began to appear, announcing the edge of the train tracks. We paused in a clearing and listened.

"Mr. Neeson came to the office last week while you were out," I remembered to mention, skimming through my Rolodex of desperate questions before her May move. "He wanted to talk about the church's recent vote to affiliate with Reconciling Ministries and to know my take on the relationship between human sexuality and the Bible."

As I recounted, I could feel myself turning red in embarrassment. "I felt completely out of my element and undereducated," I said, "I'm not through with seminary; I'm not ordained. I know what my own experience is in being (and becoming) queer-affirming and -celebrating, what my relationships have informed, and how I interact with the nuances and complexities of scripture. But I'm nowhere near prepared to engage in apologetics."

She smiled in a way that mothered my panic and responded, "What you just said you can offer is enough. It is ok to share our own stories, to provide a multitude of understandings, and to name how we're still learning, how we could be wrong, and how we've got questions, too. Imagine what hurt the institutional church could have avoided in history if we had held things more loosely and honestly!"

Under those trees, I began to recognize that, in the story of faith, simple answers might just be too small a story to tell. And demonstrating and fostering curiosity—which is often so much easier to access than clarity—may just be a means of grace for meeting completely different people in their completely different stages and lives. When it comes to our values and how we interact with scripture, curiosity aids us in demonstrating trust in the process and the community. Instead of being willing to weaponize biblical hot takes or fortify the boundaries of our camps with one-liners, we can curiously explore the mystery together, assured in the Spirit's desire and the community's collaboration in getting us to who and where we are to be next. Like manna in the desert, curiosity provides just enough sustenance for the next step of our journey.

My nine-year-old, geology-loving son has a mesmerizing, large crystal composed of at least twenty different cuts and angles sitting on our bookshelf. When I think about how we approach our faith traditions, I think about that piece of translucent gemstone. If I want to better understand that rock, I want to know from where it came, in what sort of soil and climate it was created, if it was once part of a bigger entity, and if it was formed all at once or added to over time. I want to ensure that I am not just learning from it by looking at a single cut of this multi-angled surface. To look at it from one side, it is shiny, glass-like, and somewhat teal. To turn it slightly, it is gravelly, opaque, and may contain pieces of the rocks in which it was embedded. Each turn or angle offers more insight into the ever-unfolding truths of the object in question, and to stop with one, or to reference the crystal simply as "the rock on the shelf," is to miss the rich, historical, varied understandings that it has to offer; so too with scripture and belief.

In the religiously intertwined and divided political landscape of the last decade (and counting), curiosity doesn't seem to be prominent in our exchanges. It is not, I'm willing to say, often leading the way in our charged conversations. This is likely to be attributed at least in part to the urgent reality that so much of what we value feels threatened at the moment. People are dying, for crying out loud; there is no time to get curious. We must address the gushing and emergent wounds of society *first*, we feel, before dabbling in the luxury of wonder, questions, nuance, and meaning. But what if openness begets openness and healing begets healing? What if leaning in turns out to be a more effective, more accessible strategy for the common good than pulling away, drawing lines, or knowing answers?

There's so much talk these days about who is and who isn't a "Bible-believing" Christian or church. But I increasingly find myself wondering if communities and individuals who claim and sometimes militarize such a Bible-based identity could only accurately possess one if there were awareness of and room for the complexity, contradiction, confusion, and wrestling that necessitates a variety of resources and insights with which to interact with scripture. To say "we're a Bible-believing church" feels comparable in its complexity to saying "we're an internet-believing people." What can that even mean without input, history, science, discussion, cultural awareness, delineation, sifting, categorizing, reading between the lines, and an understanding of humanity and what it creates over time? What can it even mean without the grace of curiosity?

In continuing the comparison, we will find what we are looking for if we approach scripture (or the internet) *decidedly* rather than *curiously*. If we approach the Bible determined to locate a justification for slavery, rape, colonialism, homophobia, and violent othering, we will find it. If we approach the Bible determined to locate a justification for liberation, hospitality, peacemaking, and grace, we will find it.

Just as I can quickly convince myself of a terminal diagnosis when I open Google and type in my symptoms, there is enough within the Old and New Testaments to weaponize them or use them to whatever end to which we are bound. However, suppose we—pardon the continued metaphor—"come to the keyboard" of the Bible with a curious openness to find whatever it is we find and triangulate it with a variety of thoughts, narratives, opinions, facts, interpretations, and so on? (Methodism's founder John Wesley might suggest utilizing reason, tradition, and experience alongside scripture for such a practice.) In these cases, we might just discover that despite what could have gotten lost in all the human error and history, goodness might indeed prevail. Curiosity makes way for the triangulation of understanding, a diversification of intel by which the Spirit speaks.

So many of my own conversion moments have been ushered in by unrushed people who have gotten comfortable with all they might not yet know, but who are willing to offer me today's daily bread of insight, trusting tomorrow's to come someway, somehow. Curiosity beckons us to look for language and stories instead of answers. Curiosity invites us to excavate instead of seal off.

It is an act of faith in a big, complex God of a big, complex world. And it's so much more readily available, I have found, than fixed opinions.

Curiosity may be the permission to ease our pressure and transform our liminal space into connections that feel otherwise daunting and impossible.

***

The college ministry "den" hadn't changed much since I slept on its couches almost twenty years ago between finals.

"I used to hide my toothbrush and pillow here," I told the chaplain as she gave me a tour of the red-brick building that held the majority of my classes during undergrad. I was back on campus and nervous about leading a faith-based small group for students who had come of age in a different world than I did. Luckily, one thing that had not yet changed dramatically was that young adults would still do a backflip and a half for homemade, free food.

I arrived a little before lunch to set out a pan of enchiladas, chips, and my mama's fresh salsa recipe. Looking around the library shelves in silence, I recognized many of the books that had built me when I began one of my earliest deconstruction/reconstruction journeys among the relationships of that same program. Religious *nones* were on the rise even then, climbing in numbers of the "unaffiliated" since the early 90s. I'd felt—and feel—much compassion for and relatability to the trend, aware of the "rummage sale" decades in which we find ourselves at this crux in church history, and sharing in the loosely held loyalties to the institutions that can no longer hold the same water as they currently exist. The outer banks of Christianity are where I have felt most comfortable, energized, and hopeful ever since. And yet, I worried that this new breed of college kids had leveled up in their critique and challenge of church and society; I worried that I might not be equipped to meet them there.

They had not, in fact, grown up in the same unnerving days of youth-group icebreakers as I had, nor been forged in the fires of highly emotional worship experiences. They were—according, again, to social media and the news—finding no need to deconstruct the systems of old. They were bypassing them all together on their way to the next protest for the disintegrating world that they're inheriting. How very formidable. How very terrifying. I might as well have been carrying a sign saying "I googled 'popular Gen-Z' slang before coming."

As the students sat cross-legged and casual around a dark green candle, I fumbled in my bag for the devotional I'd brought along, pausing to think before I lifted my head. For a moment, I had become aware of one unobjectionable thing. These were people, and I assumed people still wanted to be known.

"We're going to do something different than I had prepped," I sat up and shared barely confidently. "We're just going to get to know each other a little bit by asking questions, starting with these: *What's your name? And if your life so far was a book, what would the chapter titles be?*"

Some of the answers, which they offered freely and warmly, were predictably unique to their generation—a first memory of school shootings, the political hostility of the 2016 and 2020 elections,

George Floyd's murder, leaving their high school in March of 2020 and not returning. Some were familiar and timeless—the first time they realized they were good at something, a painful breakup, the moment they recognized their parents were human, a time when they felt the unconditional, transformational love of God.

The conversation spanned the hour, then we prayed, and leftover enchiladas were tucked into pocket napkins and backpacks to make it through their next period's labs. As they were leaving, I made another real-time decision to forego the semester's study plan and instead invite them to return the following weeks with a curious question for one another. Each Monday, we circled back around that dark green candle and an array of fidget toys. They'd inhale chicken spaghetti and veggie tacos and ham sliders, then ask each other questions like: *Do you think you've learned to love yourself? What is your experience with boundaries? What do you think about the idea of hell? What is your relationship with your dad? How do you know God? What do you do in conflict? Do you have any regrets?*

You can learn a lot about people by asking them questions. You can learn a lot more by listening to the questions that they ask. Centering our time solely around curiosity relieved the moment of the weighted insecurities that could accompany age gaps and the mind reading and needs-predicting that I assumed I'd need to undertake to meet young people (and all people) where they were. There is great head-scratching among leadership comprised of millennials and older generations about how we reach youth and college students in *this* time (just as there was when we were that age). I'm certain there are proven tactics and programming being implemented by those who are a lot smarter and more experienced in this arena than I am. However, I would lean against the wall of go-where-they-are-and-listen-to-their-questions any day and trust it to hold.

Curiosity proved to be the accessible means of grace that cut gently through the first few layers of our egos and pretenses and differences to usher in connection. Curiosity is timeless, never hidden from us, offering an entry point, a starting place, when others feel like too tall an order. It is humanizing, tethering, and available now.

When talking about how writers are often on the futile hunt for passion, the author of *Big Magic*, Elizabeth Gilbert, writes, "Passion is rare; curiosity is everyday. Curiosity is therefore a lot easier to reach at times than full-on passion—and the stakes are lower, easier to manage. The trick is to just follow your small moments of curiosity. It doesn't take a massive effort."

I really believe that when it comes to curiosity, so many words could be substituted in that quote for "passion is rare": Judgment is unsustainable . . . having answers is too small . . . violence is counterproductive . . . arrival is overrated . . . provisions are for the privileged . . . but curiosity? Curiosity is every day. Everywhere. For everyone, much like the love of God. Much like how we talk about the communion table: open and accessible, and right here for all.

***

In her song "Enough," Sara Groves sings, "Really we don't need much, just strength to believe there's honey in the rock, there's more than we see. In these patches of joy, these stretches of sorrow, there's enough for today. There will be enough tomorrow."

A year after that colorless day in my counselor's office, I sat in the afterschool car line with my feet propped on the dash, journaling in a soft teal notebook. The world had not righted itself in every way. We had miscarried twice since that time, the dishes continued to accumulate, and a new war now raged overseas, among many other things. And yet, I could see and name more colors in life than I had been able to imagine months before. That had not been the end.

Life is so unbearable and perplexing at times, and it's terrifying that we can become so stripped or run-down or wounded that even our memory of goodness seems like a false construct. But what if we don't have to solve or heal or escape it all to breathe again? What if we might find that a breadcrumb of curiosity may be just enough to get us to the next, which might get us to the next? Until one day, we wake up new and known, whole and—can you imagine—hopeful?

"Give us today our daily bread," Jesus taught us to pray. Not tomorrow's answers, not next year's certainties, but today's portion. As it is with curiosity, which invites us to notice one detail, ask one question, make one small, accessible move toward understanding. Today's breadcrumb of wonder might lead us to tomorrow's awareness, which might open the door to next week's connection, which might give us access to a fuller wholeness alongside each other.

May it be enough for today. May there be enough tomorrow.

***

Reflection Prompts

Have you ever experienced a time when the world felt colorless? Maybe that time is even now. What could you say to your past (or current) self to encourage the following of one curious breadcrumb into wholeness?

Could your experience with scripture and belief be characterized as one of arrival and answers or exploration and mystery? How might the world be different if more of the church experienced the latter?

What connection points feel daunting or strained for you? Maybe your isolated neighbors, your distant partner, your growing children, your conservative or liberal coworkers, your community members of another age bracket come to mind. What practices of curiosity might help you move forward with them in attainable, natural ways?

Walk outside. Listen. Look. Wait. Ask. See where it leads.

Two

Curiosity Leads to Humility

Lift your eyes up and look to the heavens.
(Isaiah 40:26)

Through a grant from the John Templeton Foundation, research was conducted on the "diminishing self," or rather on the moments and experiences that contribute to the lessening of one's ego and how a person might transcend their sense of self by seeing themselves as connected to a bigger community, purpose, story, and so on. Such diminishing/transcending opportunities go on to orient the individual to the needs of others, enhance feelings of oneness, and increase resource-sharing, volunteering, and kindness to strangers.

The researchers tested this in six ways, including one study that had participants in a San Francisco neighborhood and tourists at Yosemite National Park draw self-portraits and sign them with "me." The findings? The portraits and signatures from neighborhood participants took up 33 percent more of the paper than those drawings of the people experiencing the awe (and, I would argue, openness and curiosity) elicited by the beauty and bigness of Yosemite.

The surveys taken on the backs of these pictures showed a correlation between the smaller self and a more hopeful, benevolent, and connected spirit.

Whether the participants recognized the experience from which they were benefiting or not, those wonder-welcoming individuals added to their ability to position themselves toward the world and each other more generously, fearlessly, and lovingly by getting curious, opening up, and experiencing awe. If we could bottle such a phenomenon, we might easily imagine how our society could use the prescription.

Knowing this, it is probably no wonder that so many wilderness programs exist for trauma survivors, recovering addicts, those experiencing depression or grief, and struggling adolescents.

The popular saying "touch grass" circulates on the airwaves these days in a lighthearted attempt to make this point: When all you can see is yourself in the picture (your problems, your fears, your scarce resources, your enemies), you may want to get somewhere the world feels bigger and you feel smaller.

When I lived and worked in an intentional community (a residential arrangement of roommates covenanted to sharing life with one another and serving the neighborhood) during my twenties, we had an unofficial rule for our home. It was that when there was a conflict to navigate between two people (and there were plenty), they would work it out while working outside in the community garden. Knowing how much space we take up with our "me" when we are sitting, arms folded, across a table from one another—drawing our lines and defending our castles—it's no surprise that hands in shared soil could predictably disarm us, provoke our curiosity, and remind us of our connection. The backdrop to the disagreement therefore became the soil on which rested the place we both called home, the shared tasks and vines and tomatoes, the reminder of our neighbors around us whom our healthy relationships served.

In the Yosemite study, researcher Dacher Kelter writes, "participants enjoying an expansive view also reported a greater sense of humility, and that the direction of their lives depended on many interacting forces beyond their own agency." This, he goes on to share, results in reduced activation of the areas of the cortex that cause us to "process information from an egocentric point of view."

In another set of studies, researchers have attributed perseverance to humility and humility to curiosity. Why is this important? It is not hard to guess, in a world that feels like it might blow itself up at any given moment, why perseverance seems more and more valuable. But here, specifically, are the research findings of such curiosity-induced humility: (1) the bridging of political divides, (2) the scrutinization of misinformation, (3) higher quality servant-leadership, (4) increased social relationships, (5) the proliferation of education among those willing to fail, and (6) interreligious tolerance.

It is easy to see how the opposite of that list—any item on it—could lead and has led to dangerous realities for us. Therefore, it is also easy to make a case for how curiosity-induced humility might just save us.

Said differently, curiosity contributes to the smaller self (humility), and the smaller self is better for humanity's continuation and thriving.

***

Growing up, I was spoiled on stars.

The acreage of land where I was raised and where my parents still live is known to us as Holt's Place because of a family we knew who once lived there. The one-lane country road that leads to the only two houses on the street is dark gray and bookended by creeks in which my cousins and I used to wade fearlessly during snake season. On full-moon nights after I had my license, I would turn onto our street, cut off my headlights, and coast slowly down the celestially spot-lit, teal river of a road just because I could. Above, and almost always, a thick mess of stars spilled like dense glitter would rotate slowly overhead.

There is beauty and there are limitations to coming of age in a small town. In some ways, it is hard to get lost because of the tight web of *knowing* that comes with a population of 2,500 people. In other ways, getting lost is a strong possibility for those who feel different and, therefore, hidden. Opportunities can be few given the lack of resources, but they can also be uniquely abundant given the lack of competition. People can get bored and desperate because of what isn't available, but they can just as likely get inspired and creative because they've learned that if something new's going to happen, they might just have to execute it. I'm lucky that such a place taught me how to be intergenerationally connected, resourceful, and imaginative—the number of people who continue to know me as theirs makes up an embarrassment of riches relationally. But I remember when a rural background made my problems feel disproportionately huge. It was the stars (and Maggie) that saved me.

It had taken me a long time to find a good friend. In fact, my parents shared with me once that my junior high teachers had expressed concern about my willingness to put up with such toxic connections as the friendships I was nurturing. I know how twelve-year-old me would have responded—*And what are my other options? There's no one here.* Eventually, I began to build good friendships, one of them with Katherine. She had come into my life right when most of the tweens around me began to step into their identities, and I was getting left in the dust of my own late-bloomer panic. She was goofy, loyal, deep, and artistic. And after four years, she was leaving because of her preaching family's itinerancy.

Stuck in a gnawing will-they-won't-they cycle with a boy, fretting over the idea of impending college applications, living without language or tools for my innate anxiety, and aching for a mentor, all while watching Katherine's family car pull out of town, I felt as if I was crowding into the edges of my life. Maggie transferred to our school that year, right on time. Life was bigger than the moment for Maggie, bigger than the parish. She had bigger dreams for her future and a bigger vision for who we were all becoming. One evening, during a particularly gnarly time of being a teenager, we opted to forgo the weekend hangouts in town, and she suggested we climb the roof of my parents' house to get away from it all, "just to see what we could see."

After backing my dad's truck *just enough* under the awning, we climbed onto its cab and over the eaves, sleeping bags in tow, until we were three degrees closer to that spilled glitter. Curiously, we waited. And watched. And talked. There were seventeen shooting stars that night. Seventeen pieces of ancient light racing beyond our problems above, like it was scripted. And everything, suddenly and soberingly, was in perspective.

I thought about this rooftop during the 2020 shutdown, when the only medicine for a sick and scared world felt like it would be found in looking up and remembering that, somehow, this year would one day be a blip on the radar. As families split apart over election results, protest beliefs, and mask-wearing, as information and misinformation fluctuated faster than a regulated brain could keep up, as the start of school barreled around the corner and variants evolved and rumors of the vaccine race had yet to materialize, as the connective content that could have broadened existence continued to be stripped from us . . . I ached to remember that this too was, somehow, just a moment in a bigger, better story. Periodically, after Cloroxing our groceries and digesting way too much news footage, I would walk out to our driveway and hope the city's light pollution would be kind and clear.

I thought about the rooftop again a few months ago as my son, like his mother and her mother before her, battled anxiety more desperately than we'd witnessed to that point. We had just returned from a sixteen-hour-both-ways road trip to an incredibly overstimulating theme park, arriving home half a day before the open-casket funeral of my husband's sweet grandmother, who had passed while we were gone. To say that it was a perfect storm of unregulated existentialism would be an understatement. I worried for hours that evening that I may not be able to help our overtired, sensory-sensitive, and now death-weighted boy out of his mind trap.

"We're wonder-hunting tonight," I told him, bluffing casualness and breaking up the mundanity of the bedtime routine. "We're going to get curious on the trampoline to change things up a bit."

And there we ended up, on a pallet way past 8 p.m. watching tiny gray moths and distant planes and Orion's Belt emerge as, eventually, the sun's cape slinked off earth's edge. At one point, while I was reading a chapter of a book out loud to him, a single firefly hide-and-seeked around our periphery, and we wondered to each other what all we must miss out in the wild while we are fretting over monsters inside. The stars forever remind us that when life can't stop being heartbreaking, we're smaller than we realize, or rather, we're a part of something bigger, longer, vaster, richer, more beautiful than we realize—something we remember when we come into, as Wendell Berry described, "the peace of wild things."

I hope he never forgets feeling small in this way. I believe I'll never forget it.

***

When asked what first comes to mind when reading the word "humility," online contributors answered:

> "Putting others before self."
> "Not needing to outshine."
> "The opposite of pride and entitlement."
> "Service to others."
> "Listening way more than talking."

I think these are pretty popular, and not inaccurate, takes on what humility is and how we think it manifests (or needs to) in the world. We get the sense that there is value in not assuming ourselves as the center of gravity at the expense of those around us. Something in us knows the world falls apart more easily when humans exist in such a way. However, my favorite responses were these:

> "Softness and openness."
> "Willingness to stay curious."
> "To be close to the ground."
> "When someone sees my shoe's untied and they kneel down to tie it."
> "Humility is dust and grass and gravel. Dirty knees, listening . . . I used to think humility was static and required, but now I see it as dynamic and better shown by choice. This has helped me show up more authentically."

The Latin word for "earth" (and the root word for human and humility) is *humus*, which tracks in our language as it tracks in our faith. God creates beings out of dirt in the womb of a garden, names promises with numbered sand, heals sight with mud, and tells stories of good soil and shaken dust and clay in the hands of a potter.

"For you are dust," the scriptures say, "and to dust you shall return."

The first time I ever participated in the imposition of the ashes as a pastor on Ash Wednesday, I felt insecure over the morbidity of the whole event. *Remember you are nothing and not here for long*, is what I heard in the words that I hesitated over, thumb pressing into oil-drenched soot and smudged across skin. How did it help the world, I would wrestle, to hold space for its brevity and, possibly, meaninglessness? How did it harm to fix the value of life as ultimately equivalent to that which is shared with worms?

But in learning about the benefits to humanity that come with the curiosity-incited "diminishing self"—that come in getting low to the ground and looking up at the expansive universe, and through learning or relearning our connectedness to a longer arc and a bigger purpose—my affection for the ritual radically shifted. Now when I hear "remember, you are dust and you'll return to dust," how it falls, in part, is "remember, you are a part of the whole. You are a small piece of a big, connected story that *keeps going*, so keep going."

In a years-old meditation offered by The Liturgists, Michael Gungor shared,

"So what are you so worried about? What causes you stress? Because it's going through the dirt like everything and everyone else. It is vapor, mist, smoke, hevel. This doesn't have to be depressing, in fact, it might even be liberating. Finitude, after all, is actually what makes life sweet . . . take a breath. Recognize your frailty. Recognize that the things that feel so weighty and wearisome in the back of your mind right now, are nothing but vapor. Feel your breath. Recognize your lungs keeping you alive without your ability to make them work or not. Your heart is beating. Your cells are working together to keep you alive. And it's all magical and mysterious and beautiful. Life on planet earth is a gift, and you only get it for as long as you get it. And then the match gets blown out. So set your hearts, not on things of earth, not on the vapor, but let go. Fully open your heart to both the Gift and the Giver. The Mystery. The Beauty. That in which we live and move and have our being. That in which we call God—The Oneness who holds the vapor together—who somehow brings meaning into the meaningless."

If you've never felt them tumble around your fingers before, cremation remains feel fine and dense, organic and indelible. They are the color of chalk soot accumulated at the edges of chalk trays when teachers had chalk trays, like they had when my grandfather was a teacher. In an area of family land that we call The Bottoms, where the knobby knees of the cypress push out of the creek like mine do in the bathtub, we scattered Pappaw's ashes one winter day. Then we buried some near my Aunt Kathryn, and with some, we talcumed the base of five oaks representing us grandkids.

How does a mountain fit into a box, one might ask. Quite nicely, it turns out, albeit eerily. Mysteriously, beautifully, as it should when a full man's full existence is lived up to its end and his family lays him to rest across beloved acreage. "I believe in miracles," I remember thinking then. "Like how this dust in my hand once made life, and worked hard, and caused laughter, and made mistakes, and added to the story of us all. That something finite like life can add to something infinite like love."

What could be more miraculous? That the passing moment is the purpose—that the moment matters, maybe most? From dust to dust, I held my mortality with odd affection that day and so many times since.

"Being human," Fr. Richard Rohr writes, "means acknowledging that we're made from the earth and will return to the earth. We are earth that has come to consciousness. . . . And then we return to where we started—in the heart of God. Everything in between is a school of love."

What if humility is more than a stagnant, expected, masochistic self-forgetting, but it's a zooming out from your own puzzle piece, your single dot in the full Monet, to see a glimpse of the glory of the whole and allow it to boost your stability and trust in another person? Another moment? Another day? What if curiosity about the bigness, even (and especially) if it amplifies our smallness, is the door to such perspective and hope?

***

A mentor of mine once told me a story about an interactive activity she participated in with a bunch of other faith leaders. They had to migrate about the room, exchanging convictions about certain hot topics in the church and society. "The catch, however," she noted, "was that we had to end everything we said with the words 'but I could be wrong.'"

She shared how, at first, it seemed the air was sucked out of the room as educated and earnest community leaders milled around. To tack on an "I could be wrong" felt almost irresponsible knowing what they knew, having seen what they'd seen and loved whom they'd loved. However, as the practice played out, the atmosphere shifted. Conversation warmed, shoulders relaxed.

"I was most mesmerized," she reminisced in wonder, "how it wasn't necessarily that the phrase was changing what people believed or the words that they shared. Rather, it shifted how we listened. As we named that we *might* be wrong, space formed for relational curiosity, and instead of desperately defending our beliefs, we found ourselves open to how others had arrived at theirs."

The political climate at the time of her sharing was not unlike it is today: divided, charged, sliced into camps, and riddled with anxiety about how the news had translated through repeated scripts the intentions of "the other" for its listeners. In short, not an ideal time to forfeit convictions or chase them with a palatable disclaimer.

We certainly exist in times that require our firm resolve. It would be quite irresponsible (and darkly comical) for me to staunchly suggest otherwise in a book like this. But I think we must also remain curious about the power, societal strategy, and relational moving of the needle that can come with the humility to admit that we might not have it all correct right now. The curiosity-induced humility to learn from one's decided enemy does not have to be equated to the forfeiting of convictions. But rather, what if said curiosity-induced humility was instead synonymous with the refusal to name one person in this world that we could never need?

Never need help from. Never need to learn from. Never need love from. Never need to see God through.

One December, a few friends and I traveled to Nogales, Arizona for an immigration immersion experience. Over the week, we witnessed deportation hearings, visited vandalized water stations in the desert, and followed a *Las Posadas* to the wall where a reenactment of Mary and Joseph's seeking shelter played out between activists on both sides. We heard stories of parents who had been brought to the States as babies, never learning Spanish, now being returned to cultures that had never been theirs.

I find it deeply compelling that my home state of Louisiana—with such a fierce loyalty to place and such a fragile reality of land—is also where so many asylum-seekers are treated as criminals. With the nation's highest percentage of coastal erosion, we know what it means to be potential refugees, if not actual ones. We know what it looks like to pack what we can and leave the rest behind, to depend on the hospitality of others, to wonder what remains of all we left.

I don't know how long we get to keep the parts of our state that we so fiercely love. I don't know if our environment—natural or political—is promised to remain secure. But I am willing to wonder if there is value in loving my migrant neighbor as I love my could-be migrant self. Value in loving my "other" like I could need them one day.

"Curiosity is a willingness to withhold drawing conclusions," Amy Oden, author of *Right Here Right Now*, has said.

What if to access humility through curiosity is to not write another person off—be they a refugee, a border patrol agent, a right-wing voter, a pro-choice advocate, a Southern Baptist preacher, an ordained lesbian, someone who protests differently than I do, someone who doesn't protest at all—as someone I would never need or from whom I could never learn anything? What if this keeps us connected to our humanity, to the humus that formed us, and to which we'll return? What if it helps us stay low to the ground, from where we can tie shoes and plant seeds and see a sobering display of stars that add to our hope in each other and the day to come?

From dust we are formed, to dust we return—all of us, together. A curious thing indeed.

***

Reflection Prompts

Share about some areas of church and society that you feel deep convictions about and why. Practice following your sharing with the words, "But I could be wrong." How does that feel in your body?

When is a time that you changed your mind about a person or groups of people? What led to your conversion experience? What things in life do you think actually contribute to changed minds and (more importantly) changed hearts?

Discuss how whole segments of society are being translated by the news and social media to one another. What threats does this pose? What are some ways to counteract this with love and grace?

Can you name some positive times in life when you felt like a small part of a big, connected story? List these examples, so you know where to return next time your "portraits take up too much space."

Three

Curiosity Disarms Us

But Jesus bent down and started to write on the ground with his finger.

(John 8:6)

On November 17, 1993, the North American Free Trade Agreement (NAFTA) was signed into law by President Clinton in agreement with Canada and Mexico to create the world's largest free-trade area. Following the signing, NAFTA paved the way for US manufacturers to relocate to Mexico and Central America (through CAFTA) in search of cheaper labor, displacing 682,900 US jobs. As a consequence of the importation of cheaper crops (such as corn) from the US into these countries, rural Mexican farmers (who were not provided environmental or labor protection under NAFTA) were unable to compete with the changing and imposed market. As a result, 1.3 million farm jobs were lost. On January 1, 1994, three minutes after NAFTA came into effect, the Mexican state of Chiapas exploded into its first of many political uprisings in fear of what the new trade agreement would do to their economy. The eruption of armed conflict and displaced people continued for decades. This and situations like it have created and enhanced a current desperation to survive by migrating north for millions of people over the past thirty years.

For us, Interstate 10 was slowly illuminating with the glow of dawn creeping over the blue terrain of Arizona. We were winning an unintended race with an eastbound train as we headed homeward toward Shreveport. With a week in the borderlands behind us, I was processing, and I was grieving.

Six days before, the gray New Mexico mesas, peppered with shrubs much more stunted than our Louisiana pines, were a sight for sore eyes after the seventh hour of low-lying everything that West Texas offered. Six days before, I knew three things about immigration and the border.

There was an issue.

There were sides.

And, at that time, I probably leaned more heavily toward those yelling "no more entries," because, for the little I knew, it made the most sense to me.

We arrived at Good Shepherd after two days of road time. With air mattresses grown to full "bed-hood" and unbathed bodies, our group of ministry interns joined our host church for their annual Mariachi Christmas in the multipurposed sanctuary. We had traveled for an immersion experience, to learn by seeing, and its inaugural celebration was appropriately cultured and alive.

Following the music, Pastor Randy joined us in the Sunday school room we would call home during our stay and began fielding our first round of questions about the area and its complex and daunting issue called immigration.

"This valley is, and has always been, a funnel for periodic migration—of birds, of wind and seeds, of people. This wall is stopping something that creation has made natural," he explained. "And people don't realize that we are getting Mexico and Central America's best and brightest because of the millions of hard and educated workers who lost their jobs when the US approved free trade."

He explained a bit of NAFTA/CAFTA and how they've benefited the wealthy greatly while causing so much detriment and divide for the lower middle class and the poor.

"NAFTA is designed for those who have everything and militates against those who have nothing," Randy shared.

I had never heard of this before, but it sounded oddly similar to the US policies enforced in Haiti in the 90s that wiped out most of the country's farm economy through cheaper rice imports. I had heard rumors of this history during my time in Les Cayes and Port au Prince, and I began to question why and where in the world my country was making these deals with the devil.

Unable to keep up with the market, the local economies were destroyed, Randy continued, resulting in riots, violence, cartel solicitation of children, famine, and so on. To be sure, the US couldn't be solely blamed for such devastation in countries of origin where governmental corruption runs rampant, but to say we've had a hand in the mix for decades would be an understatement.

The next morning, we followed Randy in our fifteen-passenger vehicle to pick up Shura, a fellow Green Valley Samaritan who would be assisting in our border crossing for the afternoon. With the rain setting in for a day's worth of steady trickle, we came upon a water station set out by the more than two hundred Samaritans on the private property of an acquaintance. It was not abnormal for a migrant—dehydrated and on death's door—to be seen walking through someone's backyard in this part of desert country, they shared. They showed us the blue flag posted high above the scraggly tree, indicating that maybe help and hydration could be found there. Information typed out in Spanish was stuck to the side, giving instructions on how to call for help and where one might go. Shura explained how white supremacist groups periodically would make their rounds to these sites, defacing water stations in their child's-play quest to "kill a migrant."

I shuddered at the hatred, as its seed began to take root in me toward the very vigilantes we were learning about; I felt like I—in the prematurity of my learning—was beginning to set up camp and decide in my heart who was on which side. ICE agents here, activists here, militants here, migrants here.

We noticed the border patrol vehicle as we unloaded our own and moved toward the watering site. Shura waved like a human, like a friend. "I try to get them to be silly," she says, "because the minute we start butting heads, we've lost, and the migrants have lost." Her simple, gracious gesture—a small moment of a normal day—was an investment in curiosity and a dissent to dehumanization. It said, "I see you. You see me. Neither of us are monsters. And we're not enemies." Because the moment we're enemies (at least enemies we cannot love like Jesus said to love), we've all lost.

The moment we're enemies, we've all lost.

Oren Jay Sofer, in his book *Your Heart Was Made for This: Contemplative Practices for Meeting a World in Crisis with Courage, Integrity, and Love*, writes, "Tragically, many efforts for social transformation are subverted by right/wrong thinking, us/them mentalities, and cancel culture. . . . Contemplative practices allow us to align means with ends, transforming internalized oppression and integrating our deepest values into social justice spaces. A truly nonviolent approach to social change sees no enemies, only fellow humans who might one day join us in Beloved Community."

Curiosity, like contemplation, affords us the wonderment that looks again, that can see past camp lines long enough to give progress an actual, needed chance that it cannot get in ecosystems where the walls keep closing in to include only people who believe "like me."

Small worldviews breed violence.

Some recent data has explored cases in which historically nonaggressive, nonterritorial animals have become unprecedentedly violent with their own species amid climate-related downsizing of their environments. Scarcity (real or fabricated) will rewire us. When I am stuck in a closet with a wasp, its chances of living are far lower than when one passes me on an open-air walk. Zoomed in, we trade creative urgency for alarm, nuance for drawn lines, communication for excommunication. Zoomed out, we trust the drips to fill the bucket, the relationships to change the minds (including ours), and the investments to move us along this long moral arc.

There are many reactions to the violence of our world right now that can be employed. I'm not smart enough to know which are most effective, sustainable, or peaceful. But I'm willing to make a case that any investments we can make to remember and remind each other of a bigger world and a smaller/interconnected us have a better chance to thwart, instead of mimic, the very violence we abhor than some of the alternatives.

Investments like curiosity, creativity, and contemplation instead of camps and conclusions, awe instead of aggression, generosity instead of stockpiling, trauma-informed nuance instead of threat-based dualism, serving food to learn more about folks instead of letting the media tell us who they are, prioritizing people over profit, making much of grace—much more than anything else: What if these are not just pie-in-the-sky ideals but the greatest actions that we have?

And to be action- (not enemy-) oriented is unnatural; yet I don't really believe we get anywhere worth being with shame and loathing, hate and exile, or the retributive justice and dehumanization that come when we let ourselves be disgusted and confused, but not curious. Nowhere we *want* to live, at least.

Can you help me understand why you're scared about this?

Can you help me understand why you're relieved?

Are we considering the most- and least-affected while we're talking?

If not, how do we get closer to hear those stories?

Long-haul questions for achievable change, where as many of us who can get there together can get there together, is an invaluable goal.

Indeed, I'm not saying there's not a right side of history to be on; I'm not saying there's no truth to be had, or that all civic shifts hold the same threats. But I am saying that if we care about each other, if we care about long-haul change, then we may consider allowing our divisions to conjure curiosity before or more than it conjures disdain.

What if it is not passive, but strategic, to believe in and remind each other of a bigger world, where people are less likely to feel they must violently take matters into their own desperate hands to be safe or good or loved? When the walls feel like they're closing in, of course we're more likely to think, "Who's going to take control if not me?" There's no room, then and there, to remember that so much more is here with us. That we aren't alone.

It may be worth asking if what we're sharing, reading, writing, viewing smacks of open-air walks or closing-in closets. Are we creating desperate individuals and parties, or a hopeful beloved community with the world we talk about? If a twenty-year-old on the verge of picking up a weapon and heading off to a rally heard me speak of my neighbors, would they feel more or less panicked? I think the answer matters.

We may just find that curious, disarming questions are one of the most excellent tools in nonviolent resistance we possess. I cannot love an enemy I'm not curious about.

***

Nothing changes the world like empathy. Empathy is hard to have when we're braced for defense. It's easy to be braced for defense when we're not curious.

John says it was dawn when Jesus returned from speaking to crowds at the Mount of Olives to the temple courts and sat down to teach the people gathered there. Imagining the gold light brushing the bottom of clouds as the eastern area of Jerusalem turned from gray-blue to bright, I wonder where they found her? "Teacher, this woman was caught in the act of adultery," they said, trying to trap him in a contradiction in which his compassion would have to breach the law. "Moses commanded us to stone such women. Now, what do you say?"

I am most often interested in the people we don't hear from in the scriptures. "Whose voice isn't the loudest?" is a question that can carry us through a multitude of transformations. Here, in the story of the woman caught in adultery, I am increasingly curious about the woman herself: she from whom we hear no more than three words.

Where had she come from? Were the relations in which she'd been found consensual or a by-product of an abusive and oppressive, patriarchal society? How old was she? If she had been "caught in the act," where was her likely male counterpart? What does it say about the patriarchal legal standards of the day that this woman could be gruesomely and publicly executed while a man as equally responsible, if not more, could go free? What would it say about God's son if he substantiated the law as interpreted by the rulers and went against his own teachings of nonviolent enemy-love?

There don't seem to be a lot of obvious options to me for this scene. Jesus is cornered, and societally justified violence is barreling around the corner. Will he watch the violence play out at the expense of her life? Will he defend her life equally violently, and cause harm toward the Pharisees or invite harm toward himself? The moment is urgent; the stakes are high. But when Jesus could have done the conventional, he did the curious. Knees bent, robe gathering to the ground, he wrote in the sand, eventually stating, "Let anyone who is without sin be the first to throw stones," before stooping down to draw again.

I'm obsessed with the fact that we're not told what is being doodled. The possibilities are endlessly fascinating: Was he prophetically signifying that "the law is written in the sand, not chiseled in hardened stone"? Did he write the names of the secret lovers of the Pharisees, whom the Pharisees themselves had *not yet* been caught with, thus leveling the playing field and causing immediate introspective honesty? Was he causing a sacred pause, a distraction between charged moments, granting enough time for the accusers to get honest or get bored? Was he demonstrating a humble posture before the woman as he knelt low to the ground and drew attention to the dirt from which they'd all come and to which they'd all return?

We'll never know in this life, but my hunch is that it's important for us to keep asking. *Something* curious disarmed the moment. An invitation was issued for the armed to see themselves in the life, choices, and/or story of the woman ("Let anyone who cannot relate attack her"), which naturally and immediately (and brilliantly) disarmed them.

***

At this moment, I write from my cushy recliner in a home that we own on a street that could be described as sleepy at best, with its residents mostly retired widows. Our back door is unlocked so the dogs can push it open with their little, wet noses to go potty. My kid is at a loving and safe school in a fairly secure neighborhood. I know that my friends and family, while living their own human experiences, always subject to suffering and shock, are mostly protected today compared to many parts of the world. I am not tying myself in knots at night to distract my son from the sound of bombs. I am not tucking him in to sleep in our ceramic bathtub to avoid potential drive-bys. We are not discussing the realities of our future and whether or not we should be stockpiling weapons or rice, or if we would have a better chance at survival in another country. This is important to note in a chapter that dares to mention the idea of disarmament.

"Responding to violence with more violence is rarely appropriate," Mark Kurlansky writes in his book *Nonviolence: The History of a Dangerous Idea*, "however, discussing nonviolence when things are going smoothly does not carry much weight. It is precisely when things become really difficult, urgent, and critical that we should think and act with nonviolence."

So what is it worth when someone who is, in so many respects, writing from safety wishes to say that curiosity could take us somewhere that violent action or speech or ideas could never go? Maybe not much. That's okay.

Because there exists a long and rich history and current reality of curious wisdom from the margins, where religiously peaceful radicals can offer us what privilege can't.

Among them are the more well-known practitioners who saw the power in absorbing rather than perpetuating violence and who recognized that an ounce of curiosity cast toward an enemy would muddy the waters of who does and doesn't deserve to keep existing: Mahatma Mohandas Gandhi, Martin Luther King Jr., His Holiness the 14th Dalai Lama, the Love Canal residents, Alice Paul, and Jesus of Nazareth are a few.

In *Gandhi on Nonviolence*, a collection of the leader's principles gathered and edited by American Trappist monk Thomas Merton, Merton penned, "In the use of force, one simplifies the situation by assuming that the evil to be overcome is clear-cut, definite, and irreversible. Hence, there remains but one thing: to eliminate it. Any dialogue with the sinner, any question of the irreversibility of his act, only means faltering and failure. Failure to eliminate evil is itself a defeat. Anything that even remotely risks such defeat is in itself capitulation to evil. The irreversibility of evil then reaches out to contaminate even the tolerant thought of the hesitant crusader who, momentarily, doubts the total evil of the enemy he is about to eliminate."

Dialogue. Question. Momentary doubt. The greats knew that these fibers of curiosity, if present even a little bit, had the capacity to not only thwart the ineffective and often permanent aims of violence but to give us a way to reach betterment together. "More than conquerors," a mentor once said to me, referencing the Romans 8 scripture, "did not refer to being a super-conqueror but rather becoming through Christ something that surpasses the requirement to conquer altogether, where we all win, and no one has to be destroyed."

Less well-known examples abound in our personal contexts. In the early 2000s, a local underresourced neighborhood in my city renowned for its violent crime and drug trafficking was home to a woman named Rosie Chaffold, who'd watched the decline of her once-stable and connected community unfold over three decades. After becoming inspired by some renewal efforts in the city, and with the awareness that she herself did not have the economic option to move anywhere else, Ms. Rosie decided to turn a lot adjacent to her home—most often used as the stage for illegal deals and for collecting old tires and appliances—into a garden.

After securing permission from the lot's owner, the elderly Rosie began, little by little, clearing, planting, and hauling buckets of water from her sink to the would-be garden. She did so at great risk, as her beautification project not only drew attention to a plot of land where people were hoping to remain discrete, but it was also crowding out their activity. Subsequently, in the early days, Rosie's windows were shot out, and her garage was set on fire by dealers attempting to intimidate her into halting her efforts.

She didn't stop; she didn't retaliate. Not only was she curious about what she could create and how it might inspire her neighbors (which it did), she was curious about those characters who would, by many of us, be easily classified as her enemies. Rosie asked questions, asked names, asked stories, asked if passersby wanted to try a snap pea, asked if anyone would be willing to help with the mowing.

"Soon, the drug dealers who were Rosie's enemy became her friends. They would stop by and leave things that they had found like trinkets and lumber, and Rosie would incorporate them into the garden," writes Rev. Johannes Myors about the now widely known and celebrated Allendale Garden of Hope and Love.

When all logic would say that she had no options outside of flight, fight, or freeze, Ms. Rosie chose to plant. And ask—ultimately accomplishing ideals unattainable by other obvious and often justifiable tactics.

Could curiosity about the potential of our circumstances mixed with curiosity about the enemy who has contributed to them open otherwise inaccessible pathways to becoming more than conquerors together? Not without risk, indeed. But maybe it's worth wondering if this kind of risk is how we evolve from a world so dependent and deceived by violence into a world that knows a better way (among all the ways) is possible.

***

From the wildly popular and well-written sports comedy-drama *Ted Lasso*, a scene has reverberated throughout culture maybe more widely than any other. Ted, a once-American football coach turned

British soccer manager, hired (unbeknownst to him) to crumble the team as a vengeful ploy of the owner against her horrible, cheating ex-husband, is hanging out at the local pub with die-hard soccer fans, the owner, the ex, and his new girlfriend. The ego of the ex, Rupert, has sucked the air out of the room, and it seems that there aren't many empowering options for Coach Lasso or team-owner Rebecca to deal with him, rather than tuck-tail and leave or implode emotionally in front of onlookers. Instead, Ted grabs a dart. The exchange unfolds like this:

Rupert: How 'bout a game? I mean, we could, you know, maybe wager, say, ten thousand pounds?

Ted (amid a gasping crowd): Well, as my doctor told me when I got addicted to fettuccine Alfredo, that's a little rich for my blood. How 'bout this. If you win, I'll let you pick the starting lineup of the last two games of the season. But if I win, you can't go anywhere near the owner's box, at least not while Rebecca's still in charge.

Rebecca (worried): Ted, what the hell are you doing?

Ted (whispering): I believe some folks call it "white knighting," but, I don't know, I'm just going with my gut here. It's okay. (*To Rupert*) What d'ya think?

Rupert: You're on.

Ted: Okay.

Rupert: Double in, double out.

Ted: Whatever you say, Rupeydupes, just let me know if I'm winning or losing, alright?

Rupert (opening a case of personal darts, to new gasps from the crowd): Oh, I forgot I had these on me.

Ted: Wait a second, I forgot I'm left-handed.

At this moment, Ted throws a perfect bullseye, casually taps Rupert on the shoulder, and says, "Oh, this is gonna be a hoot."

While they go on to compete in a fiery game, it seems toward the end that the odds are stacked against Ted as Rupert's trash talk becomes more and more aimed at his ex-wife, Ted's now-friend and boss. The bartender whispers to Ted what unlikely and perfect shots he must make to win. Viewers remain unsure whether or not we're about to have to watch our beloved leads walk away, licking their wounds.

Ted smiles, loosely holding a dart, and delivers the monologue now repeated in many leaders' circles and sermons, "You know, Rupert? Guys have underestimated me my entire life. And for years, I never understood why. It used to really bother me. But then, one day, I was driving my little boy to school, and I saw this quote by Walt Whitman; it was painted on a wall there. It said, 'Be curious, not judgmental.' And I like that."

He lands a dart where he wants it and continues, "So I get back in my car, and I'm driving to work, and all of a sudden, it hits me. All them fellas that used to belittle me, not a single one of 'em were curious. You know, they thought that they had everything all figured out, and so they judged everything, and they judged everyone. And I realized that their underestimating me? Who I was had nothing to do with it. 'Cause if they were curious, they would ask questions. You know? Questions like, 'Have you played a lot of darts, Ted?'"

Another landed throw.

"Which I would have answered, 'Yes sir, every Sunday afternoon at a sports bar with my father from age ten 'til I was sixteen, when he passed away.' Barbeque sauce," he says after a pause, then nails a perfect bullseye to the unbelieving and giddy cheers of the crowd.

I feel the best of humanity well up within me when I watch this clip even now. It's an ode to the curious alternative when fleeing or fighting seem to be our only options, a demonstration of rehumanizing yourself or your enemy, or both, after ugly infighting has attempted to strip dignity and connection. What judgment, violence, and staying armed and braced cannot do is help us heal without further wounding.

But curiosity? Against all odds, just might.

***

Reflection Prompts

Consider when you felt your only options for reacting were fight, flight, or freeze. Now, consider how curiosity might have been employed to open an alternative pathway. Imagine the aftermath of all four tactics. Compare them.

In many ways, social media is still the wild, wild West of the internet. We are living through the age of pendulum swings and experimenting with the ethics of being physical people in an online world. How do you see judgment and/or curiosity on display in those settings? Imagine a reality where we have gotten better at navigating it together. What does that look like? What could that mean for us next as a society?

Curiosity doesn't always come as a default response amid confrontation or attack, especially without practice during times when it's not as needed. What curious questions can you have ready for when your "other" or your "enemy" is in prime form?

Consider the stance of someone who thinks or believes the exact opposite of you. Why might that be? If you can't contrive possibilities, consider sitting on a bench or at a coffee table (or around a dart board) with them to better understand.

Four

Curiosity Slows Us Down

And it will not be taken away from her.
(Luke 10:42)

Once, in my early twenties, when my older friends were just starting to have babies, I crocheted a small cream-colored blanket that could only be described as . . . trapezoidal. When I gifted it to my pregnant friend, unwrapped and awkwardly folded with all the insecurities of a fitted sheet, I simply muttered, "I'm sorry."

My granny was the woman who first taught me how to chain-stitch as a child. She passed away when I was seven, but I wish I'd had more time to watch how she wielded the yarn. Did she take her time with the loops and the turns in the way that people born in 1924 took their time with most things? The craftsmanship I've inspected in the intricate pieces she left us is a testament to the hours invested and skills honed. I cringe to think of her observing her passed-down legacy from the afterlife as I flopped a rushed mess of misshapen wool into the hands of my expecting pal before saying something about it "being fine if" she "takes it to Goodwill" and slinking away.

I have rushed through more things than not in my life, and we could spend a whole book breaking down the developmental psychology of that behavior and all the things I continue to learn in exploring my "shadow" side. But for the sake of this chapter, it probably suffices to say that there exists within me a compulsion to keep moving, be it rooted in a fear of forgetting something, an aversion to rest, an avoidance of pain, a hunt for dopamine, or things I've not yet identified. No one has ever named the phenomenon quite as well as Sleeping At Last did in their song "Seven," in which they wrote, "Let me tell you another secret of the trade. It feels like sinking when I'm standing in one place. So I look to the future, and I book another flight. When everything feels heavy, I've learned to travel light." I teared up the first time I heard the bridge and most times after, each time feeling more than seen.

Keep it moving. Keep it moving fast, is the impulse. It has manifested over the years in how I've read and written books, blown through projects, listened and responded, and made life decisions, among other things. So much gets done by the person who's plowing through; so much gets missed in the process.

But about the crocheting. It happens around every September when "fake fall" visits north Louisiana, and our dusty summer souls become a little less cantankerous for two and half days: I head to Michaels and purchase new yarn. Initially, I think that this will be a quaint and ongoing project throughout the season to ritualize my chilly evenings—a therapy of sorts to revisit over time, to enjoy, to savor. Soon after, and for whatever reason, it becomes a race to the finish.

"Get. It. Done," says my unreasonable inner dialogue, *"So we can be onto the next thing."*

Two Sundays ago, as a storm in the Gulf of Mexico pushed the illusion of crisp weather through our city, I found myself waddling out of the store with an armful of skeins of ocean-blue wool and wondering how fast (or slow) I'd blow through it.

On my drive home, thinking about curiosity and pace, a vivid memory came to mind of a day in college when I was buzzing around campus. In a liberal arts culture that celebrated the makings of burnout—including how much sleep one had sacrificed or how many extra course hours one was taking—I was naturally rushing around like everyone else. With my laptop slung over my back and the lunch-replacing caffeine in hand, I sped out of chapel service in step and conversation with a taller friend whose gait should have been outpacing mine but wasn't. As I subconsciously and awkwardly urged his acceleration by staying two feet ahead, he cut through the noise with a question that I'd wager doesn't get asked a lot on college campuses. "Why do we walk so fast?" he said.

"What?" I tossed, stupefied, sobered.

"We know we'll get to the next class when we need to. Can we slow down and take it in?"

I'm sure he'd never remember saying it. I'll never forget it. I felt my curiosity peak at that moment about what was around me and beside me, within me. I felt my amygdala power down in a way that it hadn't often been invited to do within the pace of higher education. I felt my senses open up to take in a snapshot of the cluster of twenty-year-olds scuttling on pebbled sidewalks amid the bricked buildings of a storied institution in springtime—something we'll never do again in a season we'll never have again. Not in the same way. I slowed, and then time slowed. I don't remember many walks between Brown Chapel and the Andress Building over those four years. But I remember that one.

I took this memory with me as I arrived home and ripped the paper off the blue yarn's belly to begin pulling a foundation chain into formation like Granny showed that little six-year-old, inquisitive crafter how to do in the early 90s. Curiously—intentionally slowly like that walk across my alma mater—I leaned in to examine the cord of wispy threads and noticed their tiny strands of white and tan and orange. *Nothing's ever only blue*, I thought, as I slowly pulled the stitches. *Not when you look close enough. Like nothing's ever only red*. Suddenly, I was back in Drawing 101 during senior year, being shoved into maturity with the introduction of live nude sketching and lessons taught by a crass British professor.

For one week's assignment (the semester's final), instead of capturing bare bodies, we were asked to craft our rendition of one single Louisiana crawfish placed in the center of the room. The only catch: You could not use your hands. We were given three days to complete the work.

In three hours, I had finished. Using toes and teeth and elbows, I painted and charcoaled, scratched and smudged until I'd created a six-foot, bright red, and clawed masterpiece fine enough for an A—or so I thought.

"All done, Professor Jones," I said confidently, wiping oil pastels from hands to scrubs.

"Miss Winn, I don't believe you are," he said, aiming for deflation.

"I'm sorry, sir?" I responded, consequently deflated.

"If you want a poor grade, you can be done. I get the impression that your ability to produce passing work quickly has limited you from pushing yourself in your life. If you want to rush through and tick this box, you can submit it. If you want to learn something, you can look again. Take your time. Because this, quite frankly, is shit."

"Sir?" I felt my teeth clench and my face boil. "I've given you my best work."

"But you haven't, have you?" He smiled warmly, which was confusing. "It's up to you. Consider revisiting the color. Nothing's ever only red."

I burst out of class like the steam of a readied teapot, resolved to take my low grade, then immediately uncomfortable with the idea of affecting my GPA there in my very last finals of undergrad.

"Ugh!" I stopped to release loudly beside the old fountain before squatting to hold my head in my hands and gather my resolve. Wednesday, I returned to class, put-out, stone-cold, and unsure where to start in starting over.

"Ah, she's back," the teacher said as I huffed to my drawing horse. "And she's not happy."

For the next two days, I crouched low to the floor of that fifteen-foot-ceilinged room where one tiny crawfish curled on a canvas drop cloth in its cold and open center. I studied it, wondering, opening myself to how I might follow my body's feelings in this process and not just my mind's checklist. Wondering what an experience of pushing past "fast and good enough" might make possible. Wondering if I'd get anywhere adequate before Friday's deadline.

Then and there, woven throughout the tiny, armored exoskeleton of the mudbug, with my head tilted, I noticed hues of orange and purple, some deep blues, salt-flake whites. What was barely detectable was red, despite the caricature of the creature I'd memorized over two decades of life.

Look again, my professor was challenging. *Don't settle for the fast interpretation of something built by colors fed to you through first glances. Look again. Take your time. Nothing's ever only red.*

My curiosity-fueled second pass took me up to the last minute of day three to complete. I've never worked harder, been as frustrated, had as much fun, or learned as many lessons from creating visual art. Never have I been as proud. I got an A on that final, but more than that, I gained perspective that has bled over into different versions of who I'd go on to become over the next twenty years—someone whose work and writing would need the nuanced insistence to push past the face value of most things and most people, curiously and therefore slowly.

I mused on this as I methodically turned the corner into the next layer of the sort-of-blue but also white and tan and orange yarn. Six rows, seven rows, eight rows in, I thought about the green afghan from the second year of my marriage and the gray scarf from that last year of college, every stole I'd ever crocheted for a clergy friend, every beanie I'd ever finished for an intern, each piece of weird Barbie clothing I'd made for my cousins, and all those single-chain jump ropes I'd gifted to my brother in those years right after Granny's passing. Curiosity in the stitching had instigated a slower pace; in doing so, it had invited an onslaught of the memories that had made me, that had mattered. Unrushed, I soaked in the awareness of how we are tied together like yarn through space and time, always more than just one thing, able to adjust, connected, and interdependent.

That blanket won't be finished anytime soon, and maybe, more often than not, that's the point. I rolled up its meager beginnings and stuck the hook through its middle. Curiosity had changed the nature of time; it had given me more time, not less, somehow.

***

Around every August, as back-to-school pictures begin flooding the internet, one caption and sentiment is shared ad nauseum: *Time is a thief*. I'm sure you could mark scrolling it or writing it off your bingo card pretty easily. Few can say they don't understand the feeling. At best, time is confusing, as in, *How did the first year of my child's life feel like six years and the next six feel like one?* As in, *how do my last two years of high school, my four years of undergrad, and the twenty years following all feel like the same length?*

Our "on this day" phone and Facebook features add insult to injury, reminding us that as we were punching alarms and paying bills and fussing about lost sleep and navigating the varying maturity levels of other humans, the world spun.

The ancient Greeks had two words to explain time, two gods to personify them: Chronos and Kairos. Chronos as a concept is quantitative, understood sequentially in equal parts (as in the root word for *chronological*)—as a god, he was distrustful and consumptive, literally eating his own children. Kairos as a concept is qualitative, measuring the richness and rightness of one's experience with and within time—as a god, he was representative of spiritual and opportune moments. Maybe, if there is a time thief, it is Chronos. Maybe, if there is a time-enricher, it is Kairos. How then do we access more of the latter in a world, especially in a Western world, that so depends on and is enslaved by the former?

The idea that time passes more swiftly as we age is not only a trope passed down from seventy-year-olds to fifty-year-olds to those in their thirties. It's also a confirmed piece of empirical psychology.

The folks at The Humane Space, who specialize in curiosity studies, shared "that your brain is encoding new memories when you have a novel experience, not mundane experiences. Perception psychology shows that you're likely to form more lasting memories in a week of adventure traveling in Vietnam than you are in an ordinary week of going to your job. So two years later, when you think back on your adventure travel week, it seems like it lasted longer than the week of routine you experienced right afterward (most of which you wouldn't have committed to memory). A time period full of new experiences takes up more real estate in your memory, and so when you look back subjectively, it feels like time moved more slowly during that period."

They go on to say, "When you're very young, every week is like a week of adventure traveling, at least more so than when you're older. Children are constantly experiencing new things. Some of these new things are really important (like their first crush) and some are totally unimportant (their first time tasting peanut butter Captain Crunch). But the point is that so many of their experiences are new, and it's new experiences that get made into long-term memories. By middle age, on the other hand, life is generally pretty routine, and you're not making as many memories. So of course time seems to speed up as you age—the fewer lasting memories you make per year, the more it will seem like those years went whizzing by."

No one gets more hours in a day than what's been doled out by the patterns of nature and science. So can we slow time in these years and seasons that we are so often convinced are being stolen right from under us? I suppose no. And also, yes. Or at least, maybe we can slow our perception and/or reflection of time, which seems just as good as anything.

Survival so often depends on systems and routines. We take the same route to school drop-off or the office every day because it's the one with the fewest stop lights. We recycle the same dinner menu every three weeks because decision-fatigue is a one-way bus ticket to crazy town. We have staff meetings in the same room and bedtime stories at the same hour because that's how trust is built, even if it's not always how memories get built and time gets stretched.

But I'd like to make a case for the power of curiosity to infuse some of these moments—not all, maybe not most—with expansion and enrichment. For cashing in a little bit of chronos time for kairos time, to buy back some of what we so often feel is slipping through our fingertips.

What if every so often, we took a new way home?

What if once a week, we cooked a dinner beloved by another culture?

What if, on the first crisp Sunday night of the season, we forwent normal bedtime for stargazing?

What if we asked a different question besides "How was your day?"

What if we played a board game instead of watching TV, or went puddle-hunting during a summer rain, or released some butterflies, or started hiding a silly figurine around the house for family members to find, or tried a different bean of coffee, or picked one thing per quarter in the town to attend, or went with a different genre of book or medium of art, or asked our family members for a kickball game instead of a birthday dinner, or tried a day without screens, or had a kitchen dance party, or let the mud track in?

My first job was working as a global missions coordinator for a local United Methodist Church, facilitating and leading teams to the southern coast of Haiti every other month for three years. There was much to adjust to for every traveler, as there always is (malaria pill dreams, the need for Imodium, and very few traffic laws chief among them). But one cultural difference started as the biggest frustration among team members but, almost across the board, became a beloved aspect by the end of our stay: *island time*.

Scheduled hours to meet translators, drivers, and ministry partners were loose suggestions at best, rather than staunchly held priorities. The running joke for most of my teams was that we were always and forever "hurrying up to wait." Without any phone coverage and with spotty Wi-Fi, we had to be creative to fill all the time between places—curiosity was given ample stage time. We'd play a lot of Spades and Bananagrams, hear a lot of stories, ask a lot of questions, and log away a lot of funny or unfortunate or beautiful observations.

When I reconnect with people with whom I shared a Haitian guesthouse and truck bed, a constant stream of rapid-fire memories effortlessly pours out about our ten to fourteen days in the country. On a normal day, it is hard for me to conjure even half the number of those memories for ten to fourteen years of routine life back home. I do not think it is a coincidence that island time (while to some could be interpreted as time-wasting) ended up feeling as if it multiplied time overall. Spending minutes to gain minutes feels very backward and similar to wild ideas like how the last can be first and the least can be the greatest.

Slowing down matters to the meaning and muchness found within time. Getting curious about what is around, beside, and within us can help us change the pace of a day and how we process and find purpose in it.

In his piece "Curiosity: The One Superpower We Don't Use Enough, And How to Use It," *Forbes* contributor Lawton Ursrey writes, "It's all about the moment, losing yourself in it, and being attune to all it has to offer in the here and now. A world of familiarity is a world where time moves too fast. That's why time seems to speed up as we age. Increasing curiosity and giving your attention to the new and unfamiliar leads to an expansion in our perception of time."

***

I think the oft-pondered story of Mary and Martha can be low-hanging fruit for making a point about what to do with one's time and how to do it. It would be easy to tell you that Martha was busy in chronos time while Mary was curious in kairos time, and that made all the difference.

I'm not *not* saying that, but I do want to say more than that.

It's easy to read the story of the sisters in Luke 10 as if set within the context of modern-day hospitality. Mary and Martha have gotten off work from their 9-to-5s and picked up a catered platter from the deli for their soon-to-arrive guests. They get home to prepare quickly, and as the teacher and his students arrive, people buzz around asking how they can help, setting out chairs and putting ice in glasses. There's equitable power and presence throughout the room, but one person has unnecessarily taken on more work and worry than the rest. As the others—including Mary—start to settle in to listen to their main guest, Jesus, Martha can't stop fussing over the trivial. The clearest lesson then becomes not to miss what matters with anxious busyness.

But they're not in a modern context, are they? The first thing we can note is that the home that Jesus and the disciples have been invited into is *Martha's* home, a rare reality of ownership that likely indicates much loss for her to have gained. Has Martha lost a husband? Has she, therefore, lost a significant level of societal provision and protection? It is a weird gender- and power-skewing circumstance that sets the stage for this story. In homeowning as a female, she has taken on significant responsibility without significant privilege and power.

She's not buzzing around the house with *unnecessary* frantic worker-bee energy. She's laboring around *her* house with *necessary* tasks. Martha is burdened yet generous. She understandably does not feel the privilege of being curious or slowing down even with all she inherited from her likely losses.

But Martha is not the only unconventional sister here. By sitting at Jesus's feet, Mary has chosen to take up "male space, receiving a theological education that authorizes her leadership." Her curiosity *and* her subsequent rest serve as resistance to the patterns and powers that exist in a world where apprentices (or disciples) were only and always men. She sits and listens when it could be dangerous to do so, but not in Jesus's presence. She risks loss and is met with honor.

Maybe Martha doesn't feel like she can risk any more loss. Maybe life is already too hard at its current pace, and all she can do is grasp at blame toward her sister, who is not considering and calculating similarly. This possibility makes Jesus's words to her feel different to me.

"Martha . . . Martha . . . ." I imagine him saying it slowly, hands on her elbows, trying to get her to look into his eyes. "You are worried and upset about many things," Jesus says, demonstrating that she is seen. "Mary has chosen what is better, and it will not be taken away from her."

Rather than the typical interpretation's sting of reprimand, I hear mercy as I linger on those last eight words. *It will not be taken away from her*, he says, as if he knows how much *has* been taken from Martha, as if he knows that she desperately needs to know that there is such a thing she can find that she cannot lose, as if he knows that she needs to be given permission to follow the curiosity of her sister into slowing down and that she's safe with him to do so.

Rest is resistance in a world that makes its money on ticking clocks and emptying accounts; therefore, the kind of curiosity that brings about rest and a slower pace is resistance as well. Risky, maybe; unconventional, definitely. Jesus says do it anyway. And that we *can* with him and within a world that is bent more and more toward his ways.

***

Despite it being used colloquially for routine exhaustion, the experience of burnout, Dr. Mireille Reese, host of the podcast *Brain Science: Neuroscience, Behavior*, says, "is actually a diagnosable code according to the ICD 10 (International Classification of Diseases)." Fittingly, the World Health Organization defines it as a syndrome "resulting from chronic workplace stress that has not been successfully managed. It is characterized by three dimensions: 1) feelings of energy depletion or exhaustion; 2) increased mental distance from one's job, or feelings of negativism or cynicism related to one's job; and 3) reduced professional efficacy."

Put simply? Burnout is stress that doesn't stop. Are you familiar?

It wouldn't be shocking if you were, considering that multiple studies and surveys now show that burnout is on the rise, with upwards of 44 percent of individuals experiencing workplace burnout, and millennials now being called "the burnout generation." Specifically, for pastors, high-risk burnout has reached what the Western North Carolina UMC Conference calls "five-alarm fire" level, with a 400 percent increase since 2015.

To understand what this means for us, we need to know why it matters.

Here's a partial list of some of the symptoms burnout can cause: chest pain, heart palpitations, headaches, dizziness, fainting, and gastrointestinal pain; increased risk of heart disease, high blood pressure, type 2 diabetes, and respiratory issues; depression, anxiety, irritability, and other mental health issues with effects on relationships and social life; job dissatisfaction, absenteeism, and presenteeism; alcohol or substance abuse, isolation from friends and family, and irresponsibility with finances; reduction in job performance and weakened immune system; and disturbed sleep, chronic muscle pain, and difficulty concentrating.

In a book that's considering how we might *wonder our way to wholeness*, it makes sense that we would look at burnout: a growing epidemic of not being well.

Louise Caldwell—writing for a leadership development blog and referencing curiosity researcher Todd Kashdan—states that "a habit of curiosity (whose components include inquisitiveness, creativity, openness, and disruption tolerance) and observation can be self-mastered and self-practiced. Once adopted as the reflexive attitude during each daily interaction, a workday would be infused with enthusiasm, renewal and meaning, all of which counteract burnout."

As someone who has in recent years experienced deep workplace burnout, I can imagine reading the above information and thinking,

How quaint. How very Pollyanna to imagine that a little curiosity could fix the hellscape of pressure and expectation and coworker dynamics that so many of us find ourselves in. I would never be so bold as to suggest that curiosity could fully remedy burnout, no matter how many articles or podcasts claimed it confidently. I would, however, from lived experience, be willing to say that it might help us survive and navigate it.

During (what felt like) a long season when my occupational-ministry role held a large amount of responsibility for a financially "sinking ship" of sorts that carried traumatized passengers, I was also figuring out how to handle frequent emotionally explosive and demeaning interactions with a specific individual. Each day, I felt like there was more to do, with less of me to do it. I found myself on a fast track to a constant posture of self-protection and reactivity.

"I want you to try something new this week," my counselor said in month two of our sessions. "I want you to respond with a curious head tilt when this person speaks to you like that. Then I want you to consider asking, 'Can you help me understand why that just happened in the way that it did?'"

The practice of the curious head tilt became, eventually, my go-to response. And while it did not stop the demeaning comments and negative environment from happening, it did *slow my reactions* and offer me a level of empowered agency that I'd not been able to hold onto otherwise. The curiosity eventually extended from head tilt to self-reflection. I found myself more frequently asking things like: *Where am I feeling this in my body? What do I need to do in this moment to move this stress so that it doesn't sit here?* This led to a gym membership and more hours logged on a stationary bike attempting to chase away difficult behavior than I can name. I asked other questions at the time as well:

What could I have done differently?
Is there something for me to learn from this person?
Is this their wounds talking?
Is there a third way to see or address this?
What is the fruit and the cost of this season?
How long can I sustain this?
Where do I see the helpers and the beauty here?
What is mine to do today?

I ultimately left that context, but I did so with a semblance of myself (and more than a semblance of my relationships) intact, I think largely, if not primarily, thanks to the introduction of curiosity as a crucial practice for navigating the woes and throes of burnout. When our pain is fast paced, it can feel as if our reactions to it must be as well, to wrestle down healing and relief. But what if curiosity can help us slow down and take a beat long enough to move forward with more of ourselves than we could hold together otherwise? What if curiosity grants us the unlikely opportunities to know love and see beauty and feel hope even in unchanging or unfair circumstances, so that when a shift does occur, we get to take something with us—something that can't be taken away?

***

"But I want to be here," those Sleeping At Last lyrics I mentioned continue, "Truly be here, to watch the ones I love bloom. And I want to make room to love them through and through and through and through the slow and barren seasons, too. I feel hope deep in my bones that tomorrow will be beautiful."

***

Reflection Prompts

What has historically been your pace through life? Are there things that you rush through, and, if so, why do you think that is? What are some ways that curiosity might slow down and benefit your process?

When has curiosity, rest, or a slower pace not seemed like an option to you based on the risks or responsibilities you face? How does the story of Mary and Martha speak to you in this moment?

Reflect on or share about a time when time seemed to slow down and fill with novel or enriching moments. How can normal or routine life hold more of this for you?

Have you ever experienced burnout? What curious questions can you put in your toolbox for surviving and navigating such seasons?

Five

Curiosity Tunes Us In for Transformation

"How can this be?" Nicodemus asked.
(JOHN 3:9)

I was sitting in a navy, knockoff Adirondack chair on our back patio, mad as a hornet. It was August in Louisiana, so our southern version of seasonal affective disorder was in full effect in my mind and body as I repeated to myself the sentence I have learned to say around this time every year: "No big decisions or declarations until October 15th." My brain can't be trusted in that heat.

My legs were sore, my clothes soaked after a three-mile aerobic walk in the thick of the morning, a third of which I'd spent wrestling our dogs away from trying to chase everything with a pulse. Over the last two-thirds, I'd cussed my way through the neighborhood, having just been defecated on by a large bird. Truly, I wanted to set the world on fire before throwing both middle fingers up and parachuting off a building into another life. Everything felt unfair, which is a pretty dramatic sentence considering I've only described to you a reality containing little more than 100-degree heat and bird poop. Not exactly enough ingredients to warrant total annihilation of existence.

As I looked out over our almost-too-long grass, listened to the cicada choirs swell like an ocean, and watched the heat waves sizzle up from dark surfaces, I made myself practice the technique I have found that most quickly and effectively convinces my nervous system that it's not in danger: inhale for four counts, hold for four, exhale for four, and hold. Repeat. I rolled my head to stretch my concrete neck to the left and then the right. I breathed again. Then I asked myself, *why?*

Why does everything feel unfair?

Well, I responded with the inflection of a brat, *because these walks are too long in this heat, and they take too much of a toll on my body that then goes home to do two rides on the stationary bike before even starting the working/writing/parenting day. Having to exert so much physical activity on top of all the pills I take on a daily basis, on top of monitoring the glycemic index of everything that goes into my mouth, is just too much.*

Why are you working so hard?

Well, I started with a little less spite and a tinge more grief, *because I'm trying desperately to heal my symptoms of polycystic ovarian syndrome before we try to conceive again while also eying the timeline of ovaries that are aging out.*

And why are you so desperate?

This was when my fists unclenched, and the tears started. *Because I can't bear the thought of a third miscarriage in one year.*

And why is that so profound today?

Because I just left the baby shower of a family member who conceived around the same time that we did before our first loss. And it is gutting to be haunted by an alternative timeline with the growing of her belly while I can't shrink mine fast enough.

So it wasn't about the bird poop?
It wasn't only about the bird poop, after all.

***

"Curiosity killed the cat" is a popular (and persistent) idiom whose origins are hazy. According to a number of sources, the original verbiage of "care killed the cat" was found first in playwright Ben Johnson's *Every Man in His Humor* in 1598 and then again in the works of William Shakespeare soon after. The more commonly known phrasing for our modern times was first noted in an 1898 copy of the *Galveston Daily News*. Regardless of its genesis, the warning seems incontestable: Go poking around in things that aren't your business at the risk of your own well-being.

Curiosity gets assigned to a lot of different behaviors: nosiness (as in asking questions to find power to pocket for later), escapism (as in being intrigued by the next thing in order to bypass what's hard), impulsivity (as in not being able to refrain from exploring the bear cave), and intolerance to uncertainty (as in needing to ask and ask to quell the lack of control within). With this lineup of qualities, it's no wonder the practice of curiosity gets a bad rap. Christian history echoes this distrust. Saint Augustine of Hippo went as far as to list curiosity as one of three kinds of temptation, along with lust of senses and power, noting that hell was fashioned for the inquisitive. This sentiment has been reemphasized countless times over the centuries as religious doubters, deconstructors, and question-askers get shamed or shunned for wondering if there is more to the story than what we've received.

I suppose most things have the potential of both of the coin's sides. Water has the ability to quench thirst and flood cities, in fact. But I am beginning to wonder if what sets sacred curiosity apart from the behaviors just described is the practice of asking the *second* question; I'll explain what I mean by that.

During Jesus's ministry, word had started getting around about his countercultural and counter religious teachings and miracles, so much so that the Pharisees were beginning to take notice. Around this time, Pharisee and Sanhedrin member Nicodemus approached Jesus in the covering of the night with what appeared to be churning curiosity. Upon encountering each other, Nicodemus affirmed Jesus as one who came from God based on his miracles, and Jesus delivered his famous line, "No one can see the Kingdom of God unless they are born again" (John 3).

I can imagine Nicodemus, on his stealthy walk to find the prophet, rehearsing all the things he would ask him once he arrived: *Where did we come from? Why are we here? How should I live?* I can also imagine that questions about being "born again" had probably not made the preparation cut. Yet, in a very stunning Jesus way, Jesus presented a confounding idea, and Nicodemus was open enough to pivot. We might picture him stutter over his words, drop his script, and follow the improv prompt as he asked his first question.

"How can someone be born when they are old?"

He is answered by the Son of God with an increasingly perplexing idea that entrance to the kingdom is found through water and spirit, that flesh births flesh but spirit births spirit, and that the spirit—like the wind—blows where it pleases. He throws in a little "you should not be surprised by this," which I find quirky and comical, like the behavior of every extremely wise, infuriating mentor from every movie that's ever mattered.

Here's where I think the magic happens, where sacred curiosity really shines onto the scene: Nicodemus asks a second question.

"How can this be?"

Nicodemus is leaning toward, opening up, tuning in. Or he wants to. He has stepped outside of his camp for transformation; he has asked a second question, it seems, not to feed an intolerance to uncertainty but an openness to mystery. While a first question could have served as reconnaissance, indulgence, escapism, deflection, control, or compulsion, the subsequent ones are where the miracles happen. Throughout his brief life, Jesus was asked many first questions by many fearful people wielding them as weapons to trap him. But second questions? Third questions? These seem to me to be the mark of that sacred curiosity which seems to be the mark of someone who is wanting and willing to change.

A clergy friend of mine has shared that when she worked in analysis for a wilderness program, they often utilized the practice of the "5 Whys" (a problem-solving tool created by Sakichi Toyoda, a Japanese inventor and founder of Toyota Industries) to access the root cause of pain or problems.

"*When we had an injury, illness, near miss or significant destruction of property,*" said my friend Mary, "*we had to fill out an incident report and it was reviewed by a whole chain of management, then we'd have regular safety reviews at all levels of the organization that then determined our policies and procedures. Over the years we had different ways to analyze an incident. The 5 Whys was a classic:*

Student went to the hospital and left the trip.

Why?

They twisted their ankle.

Why?

There was uneven terrain/loosely tied boot/they were late and tired.

Why?

Here you can see we can go three different directions.

We hike in the mountains. They did not receive instruction in tying hiking boots. The planned route was longer than the group could manage.

Why?

Hike in the mountains is kind of a dead end. But boots and route might go to instructor experience and training.

Here around the fourth why you start getting closer to a root cause. Twisted ankles happen, but if we could change some small thing in our habits and we had twenty fewer twisted ankles leaving the course per year, that's an important shift."

One could argue that first questions have a greater tendency to keep us focused on the superficial level of our symptoms rather than granting us the opportunities to tune into the root levels that lead to transformation. If we want to rage, blame, write off, avoid, deflect, or win, we might find the first questions sufficient.

Why are they ignorant enough to believe that news outlet?

How could someone drive so horribly?

What else is out there for me that can satisfy?

How can I find relief?

Why can't I get it together to be a better adult/parent/spouse/professional?

But if we want to transform? We'll want to get curious. And if we want to get curious, we'll want to keep asking until we access the deeper information that matters most.

What fear is that news outlet speaking to and what has shaped that fear?

What kind of emergency or bad day might that driver be experiencing?

Am I really not satisfied, or am I dopamine-deficient, grieving, or bored?

What is it that I need relief from, and are there healthy mechanisms to address it?

Why is there such a large gap in my mind between the me that I am and the one I ought to be?

A mantra in social-emotional learning spaces says all behavior is communication. It is a sentiment that asks us, usually in educational settings for children where trauma-informed disciplinary tactics are being discussed, *what's the thing behind the thing.*

Beneath this mantra is a base-level assumption that we're all good on the inside, suggesting there is more to the moment than its symptoms—suggesting that disruptive or unregulated symptoms are not indicative of a disruptive core or character, but of a good core and character that is trying to tell us something more. Curiosity is a protest to damnation.

There is a language for this, thank God, used increasingly in the classroom. But I have been thinking about what it means to *wonder* more generously toward ourselves and each other.

Instead of taking on shame for emotional eating, for example, can I thank and honor myself for having developed whatever tools for self-soothing were available to me at the time? Then ask myself why it is that I may be needing self-soothing. May I eventually think of the sentence "I am sad today about our January loss," and it feel right and I feel known? Could curiosity help aerate what shame could only further harm? Could it invite me into a more creative diversity of healing methods?

Instead of jumping to judgment about someone's words or choices or tone or allegiances, can I ask what I might not know or understand? Why is it that I am having such a visceral reaction? What might I not yet know about the dynamics involved or baggage buried or systems in motion? Might I have to eat fewer words and burn fewer bridges because I stayed a little more open?

Instead of launching into premature action against injustice or turning away in procrastinating passivity, could I do a little research? Could I look a little longer? Could I ask someone who knows more than I do how I might start to understand rather than lash out or lie dormant?

Instead of swimming in the retribution caused by the inner critic, could I ask in whose voice it is speaking? Where and when did it start? To whom does my subconscious think it needs to answer? May I get to the end of a question trail and say, "And if the worst happened, would it be so bad?" And can the answer be more often no, and freedom be more often mine?

Everything is data, an invitation to get more (truly) curious, and an opportunity to peel back the layers and access the thing behind the thing. And since the thing behind the thing behind the thing is where reality lies, until we tap into it, we can't effectively tap into transformation and healing. This is what trauma-informed disciplinary efforts in elementary schools, peacemaking tactics overseas, and every counselor and pastor worth their salt knows to be true: Superficial assumptions and judgments are not where birth happens. If we want to be new (or, as some say, born again), if we want new life and a new world, sacred curiosity might just be what can lead us crumb by crumb, question by question, into the depths where discipleship happens. Where love steps into its full potential by working in the plane of what's real.

What if our bloodwork was our bodies talking?

What if our news or the way that it's told or the way that we hear it was our self-preservation talking?

What if our anger was our fear talking?

What if our need for boundaries was our self-love talking?

What if our impulses or fixations were our genetic makeup talking?

What if our postures toward time were our hope and trust talking?

What if death was resurrection talking?

What if there's a thing behind the thing?

***

Most of us are aware that mindfulness and meditation are contributing factors to wholeness, but we don't always cognitively know why. We've fallen asleep more easily after a thoughtful body scan. We've entered a meeting with clarity after a grounding practice. We've helped a child emotionally regulate by naming what they can see, smell, taste, hear, and touch. But for those of us with bents toward the practical, it can help to explore the *why* behind the wonder of tuning in.

In a study about mindful meditation and curiosity, researchers Itai Ivtzan, Hannah E. Gardner, and Zhanar Smailova explored the concept of something called the "self-discrepancy gap" and how to close it.

"Self concept," they write, "is our self identity, a schema consisting of an organised collection of beliefs and feelings. In other words, self concept provides a framework that determines how we process information about ourselves, including our motives, emotional states, self evaluations, and abilities."

They go on to identify two human experiences that can create discrepancy gaps in our self-concepts, in turn creating many of the mental health struggles that we navigate on a daily basis. The first they describe is the experience of distance between the actual concept of self and the ideal self, or the gap between who a person believes that they are and the person they would ideally like to be. The second experience is that of having distance between the actual self and the "ought self," or rather the self with the attributes one thinks they *should* possess. The science they share shows an association between an actual/ideal discrepancy and depression, while an actual/ought discrepancy is more often associated with anxiety.

Fascinating, isn't it? Within the widening gap between the me I think I am and the me I long to be is fertile ground for depression; within the widening gap between the me I think I am and the me I feel I'm supposed to be is fertile ground for anxiety. As someone who deals with a good bit of anxiety and whose inner critic is frequently utilizing "ought" language, this makes sense to me.

Now what to do with the information?

Ivtzan, Gardner, and Smailova worked with one hundred and twenty study participants to learn that mindful meditation can close actual-ideal/actual-ought discrepancy gaps caused by false expectations or threats by focusing attention in a nonanalytical way, orienting practitioners to the present moment, interrupting negative thinking, and aiding meditators in accepting and processing overwhelming emotions within an experience that provides a sense of safety.

Furthermore, their work discovered the bonus information that curiosity serves as a major catalyst not only in lessening the self-discrepancy gap but also in contributing to overall well-being.

"Curiosity is linked," the study shares,

> To greater wellbeing in a number of different ways (e.g., Naylor, 1981; Park, Peterson, & Seligman, 2004). Firstly, physical health is associated with curiosity, with those who are more curious aged 60–86 being more likely to be alive after five years, even after accounting for age, smoker status, and various diseases (Swan & Carmelli, 1996). Secondly, curious people report more satisfying social interactions and relationships, and their partners describe them as interested and responsive (Burpee & Langer, 2005; Kashdan & Roberts, 2004). Less curious people often rely on stereotypes, and avoid uncertainty by rejecting those who fail to conform (Sorrentino, Holmes, Hanna, & Sharp, 1995). Finally, of the 24 VIA [values in action] character strengths, curiosity was one of the most strongly linked to global life satisfaction, work satisfaction, living a pleasurable life, living an engaging life, and living a meaningful life (Brdar & Kashdan, 2009; Park, Peterson, Seligman, 2004; Shimai, Otake, Park, Peterson, & Seligman, 2006). A higher propensity to seek

> out novel and challenging events leads to participation in growth-oriented behaviours such as meditation, from which meaning in life, personal growth and wellbeing derive.

Curiosity-fueled meditation (or for some, centering prayer) therefore serves as an accessible practice for lessening our anxiety and depression by way of lessening the gaps between the actual self and ideal/ought self by tuning in and opening up to what is real, what is here, and what is now.

I wonder how much the notions of "ought" and "ideal" rule our world at the moment, not only for our own senses of self but also for those we impose on other people and people groups. If there can exist a gap between the me I think I am and the me I think I want to/should be, might there also exist a gap between the world I think we have and the ideal/ought world I have in mind? Do the ways that we talk about society or sections of it widen or close these gaps for us? Are these gaps adding to our collective anxiety and depression or helping us heal?

This is not to say that there shouldn't be ideal selves or worlds to dream about or strive for. Rather, it suggests that we cannot access our next steps for how to get there or discernment of what is ours to do without first centering down in and reflecting clear-mindedly on the reality in which we currently find ourselves.

What is the thing behind the thing? The power of curiosity's second and third and fourth question is that it makes room for existing as a trauma-informed and goodness-believing society that recognizes that beyond the talking heads and declarative slogans, people are often in their discrepancy gaps, navigating fear or hopelessness. When we interpret their behavior as hate, we are more likely to create more of the same, if not mimic it entirely. But when we realize it is fear or pain, we may be able to show up with compassion, which means we may just have a chance at investing in the only things that will give us a chance to get out of the messes we've made. We do not experience transformation for ourselves at first levels or first questions. We don't experience that transformation for our world there, either.

Transformation and healing are found through the inner doors that curiosity unlocks on personal and collective levels. The fact that there are keys to doing so is really good news to me.

***

At one point a few years ago, I was unloading my car in the middle of an unexpected rain. In one arm was our new puppy—brought home to give us sanity and company during our COVID months of sheltering at home (and all God's dog owners said . . . *sanity*, that's comical). In the other was a load of toilet paper for which I'd traded a bottle of olive oil—a sentence that sounds like I'd traveled here from 1914. In front was my son, half listening and distracted, already soaked from the belly button down, somehow.

When we got to our door, I reached for the mail—a single ad for SiriusXM sprouting out of the box next to a newly built bird nest. I was already stressed, which feels important to say.

As I grabbed ahold of the envelope, something terrifying happened. The fiercely beating wings of a robin, lunging from the pile of twigs, scaled my arm and brushed through my hair, sending chills to my kidneys. And when I tell you I screamed as if I was being stabbed by every single one of Caesar's betrayers, I mean it.

My heart took a one-way ticket to my ears, my son's eyes filled with water, my dog contorted his body like hell itself was being exorcised out of him, and my husband rushed to the scene to see how much blood must have been spilled in such a display of drama.

"Get rid of that nest," I demanded, panting.

Later, as I was cleaning with Lizzo and Bruno in my earbuds, trying to become a better person, Luke noted, "You may want to sweep the sticks off of the front porch while you have the broom out." Good call, I nodded.

One push of the handle is all it took for a mound of some feathered mama's hard work to disappear into our front yard. Left behind? A streak of oozy yellow and frail pink fragments of shell. I dropped the broom and ran to the edge of the grass, nudging leaves around to discover two intact, rose-speckled eggs strewn about—family.

Feeling that tinge of regret that pricks the back of your ribs when you can't take something back, I knelt and began to gather the debris, fashioning a nest on the side of our flowerbed as if I had never heard a warning about touching birds or birds' things. I tumbled the thimble-sized treasure into its middle. She probably wouldn't return, I knew. They probably wouldn't form. Still, I tried because I was sorry.

I kept thinking about them over the next few days, partly because I am a glutton for punishment and partly because it all felt darkly poetic. Mainly, they had served for me as a metaphor for the damage that is done, not by fear and shock, but in the surface-level reaction to fear and shock. Which is not irrelevant for these days.

Good worlds collide. And sometimes, no evil is to blame for our suffering; it is just what comes with the territory of a beautifully tragic, finite existence—wired to end and begin again. But curiosity—or even a moment of consideration—can halt a multitude of things, can stop the bleeding.

Love is patient, they say. I've often thought of patience as the will to tolerate something intolerable just a bit longer. But maybe it also applies to the moment that falls between threat and response, in that sacred window of looking again, of wondering. Of asking one more question, like Nicodemus or the guide in my meditation app.

I cannot control what scares me—from darting beaks to a world seemingly imploding around us. But I can take a moment before tearing something or someone else apart to wonder a little further, a little more generously, a little deeper.

Sweet little eggs. They weren't nothing.

***

Reflection Prompts

Consider a time or times when you experience anxiety or depression. What is the voice you hear in those moments saying? Who does it belong to? Why do you think it says what it says? What would you like to say back?

Discuss your experience with your actual self, ideal self, and ought self. What widens or closes the gap for you?

Who is the person or group of people "across the aisle" from you? Consider their choices or convictions and practice the 5 Whys in reflecting on them.

Inhale for four counts. Hold for four. Exhale for four. Hold for four. Repeat. What's "the thing behind the thing" for you right now?

Six

Curiosity Pushes Past Shame

. . . that you may be healed.
(James 5:16)

My parents created one child who would always gravitate toward the center of the dance floor and one child who would always gravitate toward the edge of the snack table. If I described my great affection for chips and dip, you'd have no trouble determining who was who. When we were growing up, it wasn't unheard of for my brother to be invited to multiple proms at surrounding schools just so he could serve as the party starter. Yet his dance skills and rhythm, while unmatched, are not the things I coveted most. Rather, his confidence to move his body no matter how he looked or who was watching was something I would trade a chunk of my cerebral nature to have. As he jumps into the middle of any wedding dance floor, I film it, inspired and almost aching to be that free.

When my friends and I moved into our post-college ministry house in an underresourced neighborhood after graduating, we quickly began to collect a number of delicious adventures seemingly unique to that season of young adulthood: massively attended block parties in the summer, social justice-centric pilgrimages in the winter, community gardens year-round, and—maybe most beloved of all—house concerts. Some of the first neighbors that we met lived a block over and were infamous for their house shows. Since our old, nine-bedroom fixer-upper had more space, it made sense to start eventually hosting some at our place. And over the years, band vans would park on the side of our pothole-studded street and squeeze their instruments into the cracks and corners of the foyer, as a swarm of twenty-somethings would pack like sardines onto thrifted couches and scratchy floors to be tied together in ways that only music played in living rooms can do.

After our second or third time hosting a house show, I remember one of the neighbors lingering in the kitchen after cleanup, asking, "Why don't y'all dance?"

I was confused, at best, by the question and able to offer no better answer than, "Because we don't dance. I don't dance."

"There's so much good space to dance here. You don't know what you're missing," she said with a smile.

I felt I did know what I was missing, though, or at least something dormant and trapped inside of me did. It's well-researched and proven that dancing is unrivaled in its benefits for mental health as a master endorphin-releaser. For grief? For depression? For anxiety? It is not unheard of for someone who is stuck or hurting to be prescribed a few kitchen dance parties until their brain can catch up to their feet.

Still, I had not explored it past declarations of identity: I didn't dance because I didn't dance. But despite my "and that's that" energy, our conversation and her curious question sat gnawing in the back of my brain over the weeks following.

Why didn't I dance? I'd let it roll around in my head while driving, while showering, while moving housemates' shoes out of common rooms.

Eventually, I answered, *I don't dance because I can't dance.*

Well, that's not entirely true, is it, I prompted myself. *You dance quite a bit when you're alone. When did you determine that it couldn't be a shared activity?*

I guess when I stopped going to dance class in first grade after those two girls told the class I was too fat to wear a leotard . . .

My jaw tightened as a memory I hadn't thought of in years (let alone connected to any present behavior) flashed into my mind. *I had just gotten the best-dancer-of-the-week sticker for the first time since we moved cities and dance studios when another child approached me to let me know that some kids in the class didn't think I deserved the award since my body wasn't made for dance clothes.*

The scene then shifted in my memory, and I was now sitting on the steps of my grandparents' house, where we were living until our new home was ready. I was crying about a stomachache (that I had just given myself by hitting my own abdomen so that I wouldn't have to lie) in order to get out of going to the following week's dance class. Eventually telling my mother what happened, and begging not to be forced to return, I never took dance again. *That was the day I stopped dancing in shared space. That was the day I started believing I had a bad body.*

Coming of age within purity culture would take that message further—past the shame of *having a bad body* and into the increased shame of being a person with a body at all. The cognitive dissonance between the often-adopted distrust of "flesh" in the story of faith and the incarnation of Christ into a body/the Body proved to be quite overwhelming. It is hard to grow up thinking that your home hates you and you hate your home. When we (let ourselves) consider our bodies as our first and most sacred homes, this rings exponentially true. To feel disconnected from, and deep shame about, my body had taken me into identity-declaring, connection-withholding, freedom-rejecting waters. *I just don't dance.*

But one neighbor's genuinely curious question had begun to unravel the chain mail built by shame with which I'd been subconsciously protecting and restricting myself.

I have this daydream that comes to mind now sometimes when I am out on walks listening to meticulously curated playlists. In it, I am in the last fifteen feet of an incredible hike to a mountain summit, which is marked by a sizable plateau and an indescribable view of peaks and sky and light. My friends are in front of and behind me, trickling up to our hard-won destination. When we arrive, we don't talk. We breathe and we look, and then we put in our headphones and press play simultaneously to a shared soundtrack designed for an impending silent disco. Then we dance.

What a gift that would be, I think, *drenched with freedom and healing, given ultimately and incomparably by the simplest act of curiosity.*

***

Shame loses volume in curiosity's presence.

Anyone who has ever shared an insecurity, mistake, or trauma and been met with a "*me too*" can attest. Anyone who has swapped grueling stories of their workplaces or unspoken stories of adolescence, or who has dropped what they thought would be a bomb on a therapist only to be met with unruffled invitation, has borne witness to such a phenomenon. Shame thrives on statements and shrivels at questions.

In her extensive and unprecedented work in the field of shame, researcher and storyteller Brené Brown writes, "Based on my research and the research of other shame researchers, I believe that there is a profound difference between shame and guilt. I believe that guilt is adaptive and helpful—it's holding something we've done or failed to do up against our values and feeling psychological discomfort. I define shame as the intensely painful feeling or experience of believing that we are flawed and therefore unworthy of love and belonging—something we've experienced, done, or failed to do makes us unworthy of connection. I don't believe shame is helpful or productive. In fact, I think shame is much more likely to be the source of destructive, hurtful behavior than the solution or cure. I think the fear of disconnection can make us dangerous."

While guilt can guide our actions, and conviction can invite us further into our calling, shame attempts to label our innermost core with condemnations that oppose our truest identities as image-bearers of God. While the latter is fueled by judgment and fear (*I am what I've done; what if they find out?*), the former is fueled by curiosity (*Who am I being invited to become?*).

In an online post created by licensed therapist Emily Sanders, she demonstrates the difference between critical shame and curiosity by comparing their voices side-by-side in a graphic.

Sanders shares that while the critical mindset says, "I shouldn't be feeling this way," the curious mindset asks, "I wonder why I am feeling this way?" While the critical mindset presses, "What's wrong with me?" the curious mindset wonders, "Is there something I am needing right now?" While the critical mindset states things like, "I'm so weak; this shouldn't be a big deal; I should be over this already," the curious mindset offers, "I am going through a lot; how is my body carrying it? I feel so off lately; what are my feelings telling me?"

Curiosity can slow reactivity and judgment until we can be informed, until we can respond with grace. Through the years, I have recognized curiosity's liberating power as both inwardly and outwardly effective in the face of shame.

In an example of the inward, when I began work on a memoir that covered the faith deconstruction and reconstruction of my youth and young adult years, I had not initially realized how deeply I would be plunging into and putting to page my eras of exclusion- and behavior-centric theology and the mistakes I made because of that theology. I'd pulled up a chair to quite literally outline and ultimately share my years of renaming legalism at the expense of the queer community, those in poverty, my neighbors, mentees, and friends.

What have I agreed to, I remember panicking as I began to craft chapter-long mind maps.

And while wading the waters of such writing, I felt for months like my bones had turned to mush as I stared in the face of every zealous version of a Jesus-follower I had been up to that point. But writing through the different people I had embodied, and the decisions they had made, invited me out of the natural, forward-moving escapism that so often and easily drives the ship when we are evolving. And it offered me the gift of looking again—looking curiously—at what I had lost and gained and become along the way.

Mercy is the language of people who know they need each other, and there is no mercy like the mercy we must meet our younger selves with when we do the work of sharing space with them curiously and compassionately. I had been given the unmatched and precious gift of learning myself as someone in need of forgiveness for who'd she'd been and all she'd done before she knew better. Which had, in turn, kickstarted the deep inner work of forgiving others for being people in process, too.

Likewise, outwardly, it seems that every time I get together with a safe group of moms, and we (eventually) begin to ask each other questions or share increasingly candid stories, we realize that we are all struggling, experimenting, and screwing up in really similar ways. We have relatable insecurities and inner dialogues and unpublicized behaviors around screen time. In the quiet of our own bathrooms in the middle of the night, we are looking at ourselves in the mirror and fielding critiques like *you're failing them*. But in safe company?

In honesty? In the village that they always said it would take? The shameful self-labeling takes a backseat to the shared load.

Isolation breeds addiction (whether to our unhealthy coping mechanisms or our unfair judgments about ourselves and each other). Within it, we a lack systems, structures, and language that might otherwise help us to share what it's *really* like to be human. Company and questions, though, give people's vulnerability a door that, if they choose to walk through it, can lead to healing.

In James 5, where the writer encourages, "Therefore, confess your sins to each other and pray for each other so that you may be healed," the Greek word for "confess" is *exomologeo*, meaning "to acknowledge openly and joyfully." I'm intrigued by the words *openly* and *joyfully* here in the consideration of a verse often colored by the daunting risk of exposure and failure. For many, "confess your sins" smacks of the caricature of Catholic confessionals and/or sex-centric evangelical accountability groups. But considered as an invitation both to acknowledge "openly and joyfully" how we are missing the mark with one another and to pray for each other so that we may be healed, the verse takes on a more human and less institutional feel, as if it had skin to touch rather than microscopes to sit under. I'll be so bold as to suggest that curiosity is maybe what changes such a tone and setting.

I have offered confessions in unsafe spaces to satisfy the compulsions within me or the expectations around me; at times, I have created those unsafe spaces that encouraged the very same from others. In such cases, the receiving party is listening from a posture of assessment or penalty. In these one-sided admissions, rarely is an exchange occurring. Rather, a fault, insecurity, mistake, need, or trauma is being named and met with opinion or a brush-off, sentencing or pardon. Either way, shame starts to take root here.

However, when I have experienced or witnessed confession *between* safe people, the receiving parties are, almost without exception, listening from a posture of curiosity and generosity. They offer an exchange of their own questions and shortcomings; they meet faults, insecurities, mistakes, needs, and trauma with welcome, like they want to get to know them more, like they want to be known by those who are sharing them more. An environment is crafted and protected where mercy-needing people offer mercy, and therefore it no longer sounds so wild that confession would be an "open and joyful" act. Shame loses traction here, and connection shines. I have met so many people in recovery who have uncovered this gift of confession's power when met with the grace of curiosity rather than the retribution of judgment. They (and those who have learned its power in other settings) navigate the world differently because of it, as if they've learned a secret that they know can't be forced on the rest of humanity, but that they pray to God is found like precious treasure in beautiful, fallible, mercy-needing jars of clay.

This is to say that I think how we share and especially how we listen impacts the way a moment marks itself on the communicator's body and story, or not. Curious confessors will take a risk on vulnerability that curious receivers have the opportunity to honor and, therefore, both have an actual chance to realize healing between them.

***

In the evangelical, Bible-belt culture in which I spent most of my early formative years, shame had a built-in and welcomed role in the socioreligious script. It makes sense that it would within a widely shared theology, underpinned by original sin instigated by the fall of humanity at the story of creation. And though I was from an early age extremely interested in thinking about and exploring God, I found it hard to reconcile how the notion of God's presence made so many people exist as if they hated themselves *but for* (and sometimes despite) *Jesus*.

A couple of decades later, I would learn that the ideas and language for "the fall" and "original sin" were largely introduced by Saint Augustine of Hippo during the fourth and fifth centuries, and that the Jewish tradition of Talmudic times in which Jesus would have been taught would have largely acknowledged humanity's sin as a result of imperfection not inherent corruption. From the posture of this reading, the journey of Adam and Eve can be interpreted in one way as a coming-of-age story, a tale of the process of God's creation gaining consciousness, and/or a universally-relatable poem about the loss of childhood innocence as we transition from our "un-knowingness" into adulthood.

Within this framework, creation that was initially and is intrinsically *good* moves from the carefree shamelessness of childhood (imagine untroubled, naked toddlers frolicking in summer sprinklers) to the throes and woes of adulthood (imagine a husband sitting outside the 7-Eleven between work and home, relapsing after the loss of his mom, unable to get through the day without a 40 oz.). Life gets hard when we grow up: an understatement. The fears and frailties of existing as beings who house the infinite in finite shells and circumstances becomes overwhelming. So God enters our shells and circumstances through Jesus to show us just how far love will go and why it matters—that despite all that comes when we can't unknow or unsee ourselves or our world for what it is, dying is better than killing, being last and least is better than first or greatest, and there's enough space and enough grace to go around for ourselves, our neighbors, and our enemies.

In learning love from God through Jesus, and knowing God through each other, we are freed from this notion of intrinsic corruption and reminded of our baseline of intrinsic and original goodness. The creation story in this light suggests that *yes, life is hard, and we don't get it right, and God is still here walking with those God first called good.*

Why does this matter?

I think it's hard to love a God or feel loved by a God that you think hates the core of who you are. I think it's improbable that you could truly love yourself (imperfections, mistakes, and all) if you think that at base level you deserve such hate. And I think it's impossible to love your neighbor if you hate yourself.

When I was young, I would read Genesis 2, verse 9, with the vitriol of an angry and militant father. "But the Lord called to the man, 'Where are you?'"

These days, I read verse 9 and feel welled up with the curiosity and compassion I hear in the question. It is as if the AA sponsor of that once-carefree, frolicking-child-turned-relapsing-adult is calling the husband who is sitting outside of the 7-Eleven for the fourth time that week. And with merciful care, he asks, "Where are you?"

Do you hear it? The love? *Where are you*?

A judgmental reading incites shame. A curious reading incites compassion. I think one of them has a chance to lead us back to our innate goodness, while the other can push us further into hiding.

Shame is a lousy motivator.

It is, as shared by Stop It Now, a helpline for preventing child sexual abuse, "unhelpful, especially if we experience it for a long time. If someone sees themselves as a bad person, they might not see a way out of their situation or feel unable to change their behaviour. This can make them more likely to re-offend and potentially more likely to harm themselves."

Shame has detrimental effects on our physical health, our mental well-being, and our relationships.

Curiosity can serve as the antidote. As licensed counselor Dayna Sharp, of Creating Space Counseling, writes, "One of the most important things that we can do to protect ourselves is to develop and practice a sense of Curiosity. Curiosity allows us a sense of freedom, we can let our guard down and get caught up in a genuine desire to learn something, understand something more. When we can work with a sense of Curiousness about ourselves in therapy, we can step out of anxiety, fear, embarrassment, guilt or blame, and simply get to know ourselves better without judgment."

But it will take practice, she notes, as she encourages readers to imagine themselves as children, joyfully pretending to be scientists, listening and observing without critique. Tapping back into the shamelessness of the sprinklers *before* life happened, and posturing themselves as an excavator of the goodness at our cores and the cores of those with whom we so bravely and generously share confession.

***

I waited three hours in the new OB-GYN's lobby before being called back. I had chosen the location and practitioner specifically because I'd heard it was a small and personable operation, unlike the large, factory-style office from which I had come. "This is a part of deliberate care," I coached myself, "these hours are the price for the time you'll soon get." Considering how my body had not felt like it'd been given time in quite a while, the pep talk sufficed.

We were in year four of secondary infertility, and I felt like a failure. Every appointment noted higher weight and yielded scarier results. My liver was demonstrating a dangerous trajectory toward sclerosis-level non-alcoholic fatty liver, and my ovaries had all but retired. I was losing hair and losing hope while my previous medical team offered little more than round after round of symptom-studded, ovulation-inducing medicine that did nothing but wreak havoc on my life for a few weeks at a time. As far as I was concerned, I had a bad body being dictated to by a weak mind.

The doctor entered the exam room and sat comfortably across from me as I tugged on a paper robe that could barely do its job. After an hour and a half of listening and asking questions—with more time, more curiosity than I had been offered in four years of appointments combined—she asked, "Have you ever been diagnosed with polycystic ovarian syndrome before?"

I hadn't. I mean, sure, I'd had my first ovarian cyst-removal surgery at the age of fifteen. I had the symptoms and bloodwork needed to qualify. But so few professionals had taken the time to learn or piece together those earlier years and experiences like she was doing now.

"You're not a failure," she said compassionately. "You're sick. Let's get you better."

Her curiosity (and the time and space that such curiosity allows) about my body instigated my own curiosity about my body, which led me on a journey of curated care over the next few years. A lack of good inquiry and transparency had resulted in disembodiment, or disconnect, within me, making great room for shame. But now I had been shown what it meant to explore me and experiment with me, how and why to be patient with my particular process and makeup, and what combinations of medicines and movement and minutes could add to the remission of my symptoms and the betterment of my life and health. When my bloodwork came back with all normal levels a year later, I knew that curiosity had mattered.

Shame thrived on my body, brain, and spirit being enemies or, at the very least, being strangers—much like shame thrives on any of us being enemies and strangers. But curiosity plunged me into an adventure in which I not only learned anew how to love my body, but I learned, I think for the first time, how my body loves me. And that it had not been trying to be at war with or deprive me; it had been trying to communicate its unwellness and its needs with me the whole time. In the years that my body was trying to share precious and specific information, I was meeting her with statements, not questions. When I started offering her questions and space to answer them, healing became possible.

Taking a curious note out of my new doctor's book, my lab results and the stress that I carried, and my blood sugar's reaction to supplements, and my muscles' response to bike-riding all became love notes from my body to a spirit and a brain who were now curious to know it. The trinity of myself had begun to create a sacred community within me, rather than an environment where my flesh and bones stood always on trial.

And that's just it, is it not? To offer one another such sacred community through curiosity is to make the sick well.

Reflection Prompts

Do you think that God sees you as intrinsically good or intrinsically bad? How do you feel that has shaped your view of life, yourself, and others?

How have you experienced the difference between guilt and shame?

Would you like to think on or share about a time when you experience or have experienced the power of confession with safe people?

Is there an area of your life where you are feeling shame right now? Whose voice is speaking? What are they saying? Why do you think they are saying it? What would you like to say back? And what else would you like to say?

Seven

Curiosity Infuses Meaning

See, here is water! What prevents me from being baptized?
(Acts 8:36)

I come from a long line of educators with whom I lived my life by the school calendar until age twenty-one, when I graduated from college. That year after undergrad can be described as unmooring at best thanks to a series of coming-of-age firsts—primary among them was the void of a natural cycle that could mile-mark time, which occurs when you're not living by built-in holiday breaks and finals weeks. I found that life passed more quickly and, at times, with less color, less *meat*. I didn't have language for it then, but there was grief attached to such a vapid routine.

A few years later, I met a woman not too much older than I was at a grocery store. Because I am my mother's child and it was still in the days before grocery pickup, when checkout lines were like watering holes, I asked what it was she'd be making with her ingredients. "Oh, a pecan pie," she said blushingly. "I make one the first week of every October to mark the season. Otherwise, I wake up, and it's January 1st, then June 1st, then October again."

Her words stuck with me. As someone drawn to minimalism at holidays, I was aware that my lean away from unhinged consumerism had also somewhat added to a lean away from meaningful rhythm, and I had begun to feel an emptiness in my bones. It mattered to mark the moment, to consider it with care and purpose, to consider it at all. And I began looking for ways to ritualize my life in order to enrich it again.

When I first started writing liturgy, it was not because I'd fallen in love with old call-and-response words written for another time and place (that came later), but because I'd begun to learn what it felt like to not have a way to name the moment when the moment needed naming by a community. Over time, I began collecting a running list of instances for which I wished we had words: following a neighborhood shooting, preceding the landfall of a hurricane, visiting the unmarked grave of a migrant, when blessing the coffee pot shared by friends, while watching people you love drive away, or at the breathless moment of a diagnosis. I began writing liturgy because I was curious about making meaning with people in minutes that deserved more meaning than they were otherwise getting.

One of my favorite liturgists and the now-passed patriarch of my denominational community, Rev. John Winn (unrelated, though we called each other *cousin*), once said that liturgy has the power to name the universal through the particular. Which is, to me, another way of saying that liturgy helps us find big meaning in the otherwise meager and mundane, not despite its ordinary nature, but maybe precisely because of it. It is my experience, however, that the jump from meager and mundane to meaning does not happen (or does not happen quite as well) without curiosity. The best liturgy-crafters that I know are the ones who have looked and listened long enough to recognize the spaciousness of the specific.

Every once and again, humanity will find itself holding a string of words—like pearls passed down and stories retold half a dozen times—whose origins are hard to attribute to any specific source. One of my favorite multicredited quotes (whose deed is signed by the likes of Dwight Eisenhower, Clint Eastwood, and even *Alice in Wonderland*'s White Rabbit) is: "Don't just do something; stand there."

I love this phrase for all the ways that it counters the fast-paced, action-oriented predictabilities of my default self. When I don't just do something but stand there, I find that curiosity and meaning have a chance to pull ahead of dismissive judgment and emptiness. When I don't just do something but stand there, I often find that I am one consideration, one lens-shift away from seeing the broken sidewalk glass (and the broken humans) around me as capable of being generative of beauty and not just corrosion. Wonder helps me hate less. It definitely helps me be less afraid.

Fr. Richard Rohr has shared, "The Western mind almost refuses to be in awe anymore. It's only aware of what is wrong, and seemingly incapable of rejoicing in what is still good and true and beautiful. The only way out is through a new imagination and new cosmology, created by positive God-experience. Education, problem-solving, and rigid ideology are all finally inadequate by themselves to create cosmic hope and meaning. Only great religion can do that, which is probably why Jesus spent so much of his ministry trying to reform religion. Healthy religion gives us a foundational sense of awe. It re-enchants an otherwise empty universe."

It re-enchants an otherwise empty universe. The sentence alone gives me great hope for renewal inside and outside of myself.

Among so many other things, I think this is a sacred gift that the artists and prophets offer us, as the poet will muse on "*this* grasshopper," and the lyric writer will muse on "rice under black beans," and the painter will muse on paper airplanes, and the prophet will muse on ashes. If you didn't see it the first time, as curiosity prompts and artists demonstrate, look again. Look longer. Look until more than just purposelessness and despair are winning the day. Look until a story—at least a tiny tip of one—can be recognized for the invitation that it is to lean a little further into hope.

***

Some of my favorite writing is wonder-writing: musing on meaning-making and moment-marking by getting curious about whatever is there in front of me that nods to all that is beyond me. Here are some examples.

—While curious about strangers at the waterpark—

> *The universal Christ was at the water park today. In everybody and every body holding life inside its skin. I waited, well almost, for the tween on the floating log to fail and fall and float out of the picture I was taking of the next boy up, who was mine. But then I remembered how I used to look back at old photos that *my* adults had taken and wonder where those captured tweens in *my* pictures had ended up—somewhere in the world, hopefully with years of loss and love under their fingernails, with bank accounts and diagnoses and rounds of luggage worn out and retired. With lives soaked with stories like mine. Somewhere in the world, in a whole life—one second has stayed with me, all this time, in a floral and yellowing photo album in Leton, Louisiana. Strangers memorialized in vacation pictures—ever connected and unknown. I make a split decision to gift my son with the same mystery. What a human thing, these binding ties.*

—While curious about neighborhood walks—

A year ago, I took a similar walk around the woods by my neighborhood. Same cheek-chilling air, same golden-hour yellow illuminating the buzzing things between the ground and first branches, same route and water, same walking meditation in my headphones. New hope.

Peace for dread. Smiles for winces. Breath for beats. Beauty for ashes. I want to remember that Aprils can be wildly different, one from the other, for the next time an April feels like an ending.

—While curious about an eight ball—

From this Minecraft-wrapped, Squishmallow-covered bedside, I can see an eight ball, a cyborg hand, and a million chapter books and small containers of slime. The LEGOs are toward the top because they've lost priority as he's gained inches. The lighting in this room after dinner looks like the yellow-shadowed lighting from my own childhood after-dinner bedroom, and I am reminded that I'll never live there again and that one day he'll say the same. I scanned through my mom's countless emailed recipes today looking for her pork chop casserole, keenly aware of how long it must have taken her a couple of years ago to type them all out. Time folded for a second and I felt a jump-scare at the thought of how I'll scroll through these when she's gone and, well, they're more than recipes, aren't they? This air feels randomly tender until Facebook memories remind me that Aunt Kathryn's been gone for thirteen years today, and I wonder again if she's rocking my parents' grandbaby like my parents rocked hers. I'm placing things into a forward and backward time capsule—that eight ball, these emails, this memory, those ashes—with the fear and trembling and wonder of sweet, weird, fleeting days. To look on this evaporating boy with such impossible love, to remember being nine like it wasn't a hundred becomings and losses and expansions ago, to know I have been impossibly loved while evaporating, too . . . human, haunting, holy.

—While curious about an old man—

An old man sat in Jason's Deli waiting,
phoneless,
for his kids? grandkids? to order
his food and theirs.
He watched all the people
buzz and bump with eyes
half pity, half precious.
I wondered if he wondered
if we all know
what matters.

—While curious about driving away—

Blessed are the homesick
for they know what they're missing.
What a lucky pain.

—While curious about tragedy—

I have come to a simple revelation in that, through all the tragedies I have borne, witnessed, or feared, instead of asking "Where is God?" I could have been asking, "Where is love?" If God is Love, then God is wherever love is in tragedy. But rather than this, I have most often asked, "Where is certainty?"

When life feels like too much or too fast, when words and connection are needed most, curiosity-infused meaning has been a grace unto itself. Mercy of mercies, we don't have to look far to find it.

***

Curiosity-infused meaning is sacramental.

The story of our faith makes great room for curiosity where bread is more than bread; wine is more than wine; water is more than water; fish and light and oil and bodies and graves and trees and tables are all more than how they're superficially understood. If curiosity beckons *what's the thing behind the thing*, then there is a case to be made that curiosity is at the heart of a sacramental life.

By the time readers of the book of Acts get to chapter eight, the followers of the way of Jesus have indeed been thrust out of the honeymoon period for their new movement. Not only have Stephen and six other servants been chosen and commissioned by the disciples to care for the body while they are out spreading the message of love, but Stephen has been seized and stoned in an execution sanctioned by the then-named Saul.

"And there arose on that day a great persecution against the church in Jerusalem," the scriptures say, "and they were all scattered throughout the regions of Judea and Samaria, except the apostles." One might assume that this time of fast change and panic would not have left much room for making meaning.

During this urgent and scattered time, an angel appeared to Phillip and instructed him to "get up and go" down from Jerusalem to Gaza, the author of Acts noting that this was "a desert place"—which is to say, it was an unlikely environment for growth and thriving, but also it was the wilderness, which is a "site of transformation, where the stranger becomes friend, the outsider becomes an insider." Along this journey, he came across a chariot where an Ethiopian eunuch in the service of Queen Candace was reading the prophet Isaiah on a return route from worshipping in Jerusalem.

Here, we are invited to hone in on this story's main character. In fact, Elton Sherwin, in his podcast episode "The Baptism of the Ethiopian Eunuch," points out that stories of great significance in the Bible begin with the same commission as Phillip's to *get up and go* (this occurs with Abraham, Moses, Micah, the healed paralytic, and Saul); and stories of great significance in the Bible end with the spirit of God carrying people away. Therefore, maybe one of the first things we can recognize is that here is a story bookended in such a way that suggests it is worth our attention. This story about this eunuch is important.

And while we may be tempted to read the matter-of-fact naming of eunuchs in the Bible as if they held a very normalized and accepted role in society, many researchers believe that eunuchs were a generalized third gender (possibly encompassing those who were castrated, infertile, intersex, and so on) and considered sexually *other* and socially marginalized. When the story finds the eunuch, he is likely fresh off of facing the reality of his own religious rejection, as he would have been excluded from worship within the Jerusalem temple (Deut 23:1).

"Go over and join his chariot," the Spirit told Phillip, who was listening.

Phillip asked the eunuch if he understood what he was reading. The eunuch curiously invited Phillip's company and guidance, and Phillip went on to tell him "the good news about Jesus" (verse 35). The eunuch then asked questions whose answers would increase his confidence in his worth in God and God's story. And knowing that such a moment of worth should be marked, he gestured toward the very normal water along the road.

"See, here is water!" the eunuch said. "What prevents me from being baptized?" Then, after stopping the chariot, they both descended into the water. And bookended by significance, the story of the first gentile baptism (the head of the family tree for those of us who consider ourselves baptized gentiles) was that of the once-excluded, societally marginalized, sexual other.

Among other things, this story reminds us that we are more than what the world says we are; our lives are more than what we've been told they are, as the water is more than water. It is our new existence and rightful place within a love that has enough room for all. Within a love that can re-enchant.

Curiosity crosses lines that inhibit meaning-making, moves us into territory where the last gets to be first, and very ordinary elements get to mark extraordinary inclusion.

***

I entered childbirth rigid and unprepared, unwilling to lose control or embrace the inevitable changes to my capacity, lifestyle, and mental processing. When I found out we would be having our son, my primary loyalty and most of my hours were being dedicated to my idealistic commitment to world betterment through all-consuming ministry. I was determined for very little to change and for parenthood to fold seamlessly into the rhythm and responsibilities of life before conception.

I don't imagine that many, if any, of us can be completely prepared for parenthood.

Postpartum depression came more like an infection than a virus—growing unsuspectingly and dangerously rather than suddenly. I had never before experienced such bone-deep levels of hopelessness compounded with impossible exhaustion and the spiral of having to eat my words and reassess all the things I'd sworn I would or wouldn't do as a parent. My body, brain, and spirit had limits that I'd not before encountered and by which, in all honesty, I didn't love feeling bound. It felt like a lot of parts of myself that I'd confidently told people would live forever were dying faster than I could salvage them. I can't even imagine what I would have done if I'd not become friends with Katie in this season.

There is no feeling like that of the sun going down when you are in the early days of caring for infants—when your body begins to register that the rest of the world is about to leave you for the next eight hours. But like a lifeline for my soul, Katie was a friend of a friend who happened to be up nursing her own newborn in the same hours that I was awake, struggling to nurse mine. And we connected over texts. Soon, our separate despair became fodder for shared stories. Curious messages—like skillfully folded notes shoved into friends' lockers between classes—would be waiting for me in my inbox between wake ups, asking things like, *What did y'all have for supper?* And *Did you watch the latest SNL?* And *Have you hallucinated that the diaper bin is a Pomeranian yet?* And *Do you miss what life was like before?* I'd answer, then leave more questions "one locker over" for the next feeding.

Not too long after, we decided to take our shared stories to a shared blog and began to connect more widely with new parents who were all, it seemed, figuring it out the hard way like we were. When we moved the richness of those questions and answers and considerations online, it felt like the pain and growth and misfortune that we were constantly encountering in the newness of motherhood now had a bigger purpose, which colored the experiences with meaning. Curiosity had helped life (or transition, or the death of something) feel less like it was happening *to us* and more like a story to explore and connect over. When my son peed in his own ear, or I got a throat infection after improperly using a nasal suction device, or I went back to work, or I started taking an SSRI, or we pivoted away from cloth diapers, breast-only feeding, and solely homemade and organic baby food to save our sanity, the mini-deaths were not just losses but invitations into shared and meaningful life-again.

We've since closed the blog, while remaining dear friends as those babies now skirt the edge of junior high. But I know, deep in the pit of my person, that life after the death of who I'd been depended on the friendship and meaning made possible by curiosity.

A few years later, a loved one of mine was navigating her own experience with postpartum depression, and I recognized the signs. Across the breakfast bar at my parents' house, she said, almost as if to no one, "I've been thinking things like *what's all of this for if not to just pay bills and die?*"

Though these particular examples come largely from the fruit of exhaustion and hormones and life change, they nod to a very universally human ache. We long for things to matter.

"A growing body of research," psychology researchers Routledge and FioRito write, "identifies meaning in life as a fundamental human need that strongly influences both psychological and physical well-being. Individuals who perceive their lives as full of meaning live longer, healthier, and happier lives than those less inclined to view their lives as meaningful. . . . More specifically, we argue that meaning functions as a self-regulatory and motivational intrapsychic resource that orients people toward the types of cognitions and behaviors that build and sustain healthy communities and societies."

Mattering matters, their study suggests, not only for our own personal well-being but for the well-being of our communities. This cricket mattering, this minute mattering, the outsider mattering, the bread crumbling as it dips into the juice mattering *matters*. Curiosity helps us not just do something, but stand there long enough to recognize the magic in the mundane moment—even this one.

***

Reflection Prompts

What rituals, big or small, help you to mark the moment or the season?

Consider a time for which you wish you'd had words for a community to use. Write a simple two-line, call-and-response liturgy for that moment. Share as you feel moved.

Think about and/or discuss the significance of the Ethiopian eunuch's baptism. Follow your curiosity about the story.

Are there parts of or places in your life that ache for re-enchantment and meaning-making? How might not doing something but standing there and getting curious contribute to such precious ends?

Eight

Curiosity Connects Us

He broke it and gave it to his disciples.
(MATTHEW 26:26)

I sat on an upside-down five-gallon bucket wearing an ankle-length skirt and T-shirt on a day that felt more brisk than what I'd imagined for Kenya. My friend, another bleeding-heart college student on the mission trip, sat on the other side of a hunter-green mesh covering we were sewing for one of the women's center's countless windows. We weren't familiar with the colonizing history of mission efforts yet, nor of how we were or weren't participating in "voluntourism." It would be a couple of countries and years later before we began to ask those questions. However, we were comically aware that we'd flown 8,500 miles for nearly as many dollars to sew mosquito netting.

For hours, for days, we would leave morning and afternoon tea under palmed pavilions to perch atop those buckets. I would push a tiny needle laced with fishing wire through a minuscule hole. My friend would catch it, thread it, loop it, and push it right back through. Repeat and repeat and repeat and repeat. It was inefficient at best, yet the volley of the thing made the repairs more possible (and the malaria less probable). When I think about how curiosity connects us, I think about this moment—it's the exchange that binds us.

On the back lot of a no-cost health center and pharmacy in my city, a bright and detailed mosaic mural spreads prominently across a wall in full color. Its message, which reads "Beloved Community," was an effort of thousands of neighbors and partners working over six months under the guidance of a local ceramicist. At the time, I served as the director of an arts nonprofit, facilitating the ceramicist's work and grant-funding. From that vantage point, I had the behind-the-scenes privilege of helping with project prep. With great care and countless hours, she would roll out the smooth and thin slabs of umber clay, cut them into tiny and varied tiles, and then use carving tools to etch each of their backs before drying, painting, firing, and adhering.

"This part feels . . . tedious," I said, opting for an alternative word to *soul-destroying*. "Why are we adding grooves to all of these?"

Patiently and like a good teacher, she said, "The grooves are how they stick. We'll similarly texture the wall where they'll go, and then their binding will be more secure because they'll have attached *into* each other rather than just *onto* each other." When I think about how curiosity connects us, I think about this moment—it's the exchange that secures us.

And such exchanges do not occur without vulnerability and exposure—without offering *and* welcoming the needle or the carving tool or the shared life.

Improv comics know this secret better than most.

"The roots of improvisational theatre are found in the games developed in the 1920s by Viola Spolin, a social worker helping immigrant children communicate with each other on Chicago's South Side. Viola's son, Paul Sills, was a co-founder of The Second

City—home to comedic legends such as Tina Fey, Stephen Colbert, Steve Carell and Keegan-Michael Key. Great improvisers continually practice empathy and curiosity through simple improv games that focus on listening and building upon the ideas of others."

Improv, at its best, is the art of receiving another's content while staying committed to accepting and adding to that content, rather than blocking or berating it. An improv professional is dedicated to the art of "yes, and" rather than "no, but." They riff; they don't punt. They play and pivot curiously and bravely; they don't judge or judgmentally and insecurely withhold. Nothing supports improv like curiosity, whose very nature says, "You put yourself out there. I will now curiously receive it and curiously consider how I might add to it and return it to you with similar vulnerability and trust."

This is how a solid bit gets "feet," a mesmerizing game goes into overtime, a lasting relationship gets reimagined, and a meaningful prayer finds its way into the depths of our souls: with the connection that comes from an openness that comes from a curious posture toward another. In his book *Becoming the Answer to Our Prayers*, activist, author, and co-founder of the Red Letter Christians movement Shane Claiborne wrote of his former mentor, "Mother Teresa was once asked in an interview, 'What do you say when you pray?' She replied, 'Nothing, I just listen.' So then the reporter asked, 'Well then, what does God say to you?' Her answer: 'Nothing much, He just listens.'" When I think about how curiosity connects us, I think about this response—it's the exchange that creates belonging.

I had been living in Washington DC for nearly half a summer when my southern parents came to visit. Checking my mom's first-ever flight off her bucket list, they traveled to see their college sophomore daughter's blow-up mattress living quarters in the barred rooms of a Sunday school annex in the northwest quadrant of the nation's capital. I loved so much about my months in DC and the opportunities I was given through a service organization to learn a beloved side of the city that most tourists will never see. My coworkers, the youth we were leading, and I spent hours in the parks and shelters, learned the Mall like the back of our hands, and grew to hold space for the profundity of the powerful and the underprivileged, sharing such close proximity in the seat of world influence. I came to have a favorite pizza walk-up, a favorite laundromat, and a favorite spot to sit at the Lincoln Memorial. I read perspective-changing books and had perspective-changing conversations while there. If asked about an example of my own coming-of-age chapter, I think of Washington. I gained so much from those months of steep cultural learning curves. And . . . I lost my natural ability to talk to strangers.

Maybe it was the fast-paced schedules of our service weeks or the fast-paced walking of thousands of business-clad pedestrians, but for better or worse, I'd started keeping to myself while out and about in the bustling city. I stopped asking questions, and I didn't realize it until my parents arrived.

So that they could lay eyes on my living quarters and meet my ministry partners, they'd offered to take a cab from their hotel to pick me up for dinner. As we folded back into our seats, I succinctly and with the tone of someone who'd like to get to the point, and no further, stated the destination to the driver before leaning back to buckle.

To my shock (and my shock at my shock) and utter mortification, one of my parents broke the fourth wall of the car by asking with such friendship, "What's your name, sir?"

We don't do that here, I thought with alarm.

And with immediate and genuine joy, the driver shared his name and where he was from, what brought him to DC and what his life consisted of outside of shuttling folks from place to place. His sharing turned into questions, which turned into my parents' sharing, and so forth. And I realized by the end of our transit that I felt less alone in DC and more hopeful for the world.

When I think about how curiosity connects us, I think about this cab ride—it's the exchange that binds us. Curiosity had brought home to us in a distant place.

Curiosity had demonstrated a vulnerability and invited an interdependence, if even just brief, that mattered—mattered to the moment and mattered enough in the moment to matter all these years later, too.

***

There's a whole section of TikTok dedicated to videos about hiding from people who are knocking on your front door. Most of them are captioned with things like "millennials when someone unexpectedly rings the doorbell," and they all contain embarrassingly relatable examples of people belly-crawling away from windows, scurrying to review Ring footage, or rolling off of couches and into adjacent rooms.

I'm not sure whether this phenomenon can be blamed on dwindling social skills or is simply the result of our increasingly digital age. The combination of unpredictable salespeople, religious proselytizing, crime anxiety, and our texting culture's preference for announcing arrivals with "here!" has shaped our modern behavior. As a result, life has migrated from the front porch to the back, and doorbells are now experienced as aggressive intrusions. This is to say nothing of what we were conditioned by COVID to normalize regarding the safety of our closed doors and distance from strangers. I wonder what the cost of such societal shifts has been.

According to Pew Research, only 57 percent of Americans know *some* of their neighbors while 23 percent of adults under thirty don't know any at all. Given the benefits of well-connected neighborhoods—including fewer lives lost to traumatic events like natural disasters and mass shootings, lower rates of crime and gun violence, and generally boosted well-being, health, and joy—we can clearly see what disconnection costs us.

But accessing said benefits comes with exposure, with vulnerable risk. To know my neighbor, to know my cab driver, to (truly) know my friends and family members and coworkers, I have to open myself up. Like with the carving of clay grooves, the opening of doors allows us the opportunity to become a part of one another.

"On the first day of the Festival of Unleavened Bread," it says in Matthew 26:17, "the disciples came to Jesus and asked, 'Where do you want us to make preparations for you to eat the Passover?'"

Jesus instructed his disciples to go into Jerusalem and tell a man that his "appointed time is near" and that he'd like to celebrate the Passover with his followers at the man's house. I want to know so much more about this homeowner. Had Jesus already had a conversation with him so that he could be anticipating such an appointed time? Had he been a listener, follower, or patron in any of the previous stories? Was he so tuned into the Spirit that he would have just known what this meant with no prior knowledge? Regardless, I am moved by his vulnerable willingness and neighborly welcome to allow the incarnate God space and time to connect with his closest people over a meal that would have ripple effects throughout culture and millennia.

I imagine the mood was somber around the table. It was no secret that Jesus was quickly becoming an enemy of the state, and whether his followers grasped the events ahead of them or not, surely there was an energy suggesting that threat was imminent. "While they were eating," the scripture says, "Jesus took the bread, and when he had given thanks, he broke it and gave it to his disciples, saying, 'Take and eat; this is my body.'"

The Greek for "broke/break" here is *klaio*, and my favorite definition of the word says "to break, but in the sense of arresting some natural progression and directing its energy into a bursting delta of fragments, streams, branches, etc." Living in a river state, I can appreciate the visual of a bursting delta, where the waters of the rushing Mississippi shoot out and spread through the larger body, becoming a part of the Gulf by feeding the whole. The delta here is a liminal space, where salt and sediment mix, where lines are blurred and change happens. It's also often fertile with nutrients as this is the site where the silt builds up.

Where the one breaks into the many, transformation and growth are most possible.

I think about that fishline needle, those clay grooves, and that cab drive when I think about the bread that the disciples took into their bodies and the bread that I take into mine every time the loaf is torn on Sunday mornings and I am subsequently invited to give my own life away. In this sacramental mystery of our faith, I am connected into (rather than simply onto) the longer story of redemption and its people.

It may be odd to consider that the fruit of communion could translate directly to an open front door, but what if? What if my own life could have its natural progression arrested and energy directed into a bursting delta of transformative and fertile interactions, all thanks to what is happening on my own porch? What if *klaio* was ushered in by the curiosity of a turned lock and a first and second question?

While TikTok gets saturated with doorbell-hiding videos (and no shade since I slinked away from mine like a ferret just last week), whole pockets of the world are curiously experimenting with alternatives.

Some folks are planting front "yardens," or rows of fruit trees complete with signs inviting passersby to share in the harvest.

In certain neighborhoods, people set up free lemonade stands or inflatable movie projection in their yard and invite the rest of the block to stroll over.

Through online community-focused apps or social media, neighbors are creating assets and skills directories that can be used at normal times but become especially helpful during times of crisis or concern.

Kristen Schnell, the founder of The Turquoise Table and Front Yard People Movement, set out to break the isolation and monotony of life by getting to know her neighbors at a turquoise picnic table stationed in her front yard. "Today, there are Turquoise Tables all across America, from California to Maine. In all fifty states and in thirteen countries, Turquoise Tables have become a symbol of hospitality, a safe place to sit down and connect over a cup of coffee or glass of sweet tea."

As the weather starts to feel less like hell itself in north Louisiana, I find myself wondering how a front-yard picnic table and a simple "if you see us out, stop by" on our block's Facebook page might skew the isolated evening doldrums and add to connection. I find myself wondering how that connection might add to wholeness, well-being, and a better world. Might it be similar to an improv line thrown out vulnerably and curiously, with the trust that it will be accepted and added to, and the hope that the binding that is only possible through such means will be exponentially worth it, like feeder waters and broken bread?

***

But the vulnerability that's initiated by curiosity and that can lead to deep and necessary connection can be terrifying. What if I ask one too many questions about my faith and it leads to a risky doubt? What if I try to get to know someone and am rejected? What if I open my front door and am met with ill intentions? What if I start to explore my inner world and experience a rewounding?

I feel it's fair to assume that we avoid vulnerability, and therefore are suspicious of the curiosity that leads to it, because we fear death and loss. This on some real levels is understandable and, we assume, evolutionary. Since the late 1800s at least, the idea of "survival of the fittest" has permeated our science, history, and sociological conversations. Those with the most muscles and money and the least mistakes get ahead. To inherit or expose weakness is to invite threat.

I grew up on farmland about an hour from where I live now, where my Pappaw raised cattle and grew more rows of purple hull peas than we ever had hands to shell. At some point in elementary school, he and my parents bought me an incubator and a few half-dollar-sized eggs to watch do absolutely nothing for about twenty days before tiny, pale beaks would begin poking pinholes through their casing. The strong-legged chicks would burst through their little porcelain armor with great force and zest before naturally finding their water and food bowls like pros. But every now and then, a newborn would get stuck mid-crack. And I would find their fuzzy forms heaving with labored breath, surrendered to their fate in a corner of the brooder. Death- and weakness-averse chicken-raising (and a strict survival-of-the-fittest posture) might register such a scene as a failure meriting a culling.

As I reflect on the hundreds of chickens we'd go on to hatch, raise, and breed, it's the vulnerable ones that I connected with most. Real bonds were formed as I pulled tiny specks of shells off of sticky down, dunked baby beaks into water then grain over and over again until they could learn to smack on their own, and made sure the chicks didn't leave the warmth of the red lamp light too quickly or until they could integrate uniquely into their environment.

I'm not saying I had favorites, but her name was Lucy. And I'll tell you now that if a fox had gotten into the house that she shared with dozens of her siblings, I can assure you which fowl would get my first and fiercest protection, because we had bonded. Her vulnerability, not the alternative, had connected us, *adding to* rather than *diminishing* her chances of survival. She didn't need to be perfect or competitive to sustain herself in a setting where we were curious enough about each other to care.

But baby chickens stuck in shells sound quaint and low stakes, like a charming metaphor, when compared to the real threats, differences, and changes that we actually experience in the world. I have spoken to good, loving, generous people in the last couple of years who are terrified about what they are hearing is happening at the border. I can understand how three minutes spent on the big news outlets can color their opinion. The outrage getting commodified and wielded across lines for political control is disturbing, contradictory, and confusing. Mostly, I have been thinking about how the hot takes don't make us more curious about God in each other; they don't help me love my neighbor more, which we say is the whole point of the point.

Years after Kenya, and toward the end of my tenure as a church's global outreach director whose sole work was with teams and partners in Haiti, I traveled one last round to the southern coast of Les Cayes, this time with a group of college students, their professors, and a handful of young adults. My employment was taking me into new opportunities while my faith was taking me into deeper dissections of what help and harm we were contributing to while in-country. I'd made a lot of mistakes in muddying the waters of power dynamics and cross-cultural investment, and I'd found exploitative adventure in foreign stories where I could be good because someone was in need. But I also learned the impact of perspective and stories, I witnessed constant willingness to pivot to doing better each time we knew better, and I saw person after person link their lives—both briefly and indefinitely—to the Haitian people and land.

I was beyond grateful that my last trip was in partnership with two agnostic professors of language and philosophy, whose questions were not clouded by the Christian missions-speak of my world. Together, we designed our travels as a service-learning, class-credit trip rooted in an education exchange intended to be as edifying and low-footprint as possible. The students would share about Louisiana history, then the locals would share about Haitian history. The students would teach the children how to use tools that we'd brought, then the children would teach us how to Rara dance. The students would outline the information we'd come with regarding their new water cleaning system, then the mamas would show us how to carry said water on our heads. It had been one thing to be curious about my experience in their country all those years leading up to the last; it was another to be curious about theirs. Needle-in, needle-out binding.

Evens was a beloved translator I'd gotten to know on trips before, and now by the end, was a friend to all. He worked with us at multiple guesthouses and orphanages, interpreted countless conversations for dozens of partnerships and pivots. He advocated fiercely during some of our toughest work on behalf of sick children. He opened his home and his family to us, introduced us to street food, was patient as we practiced the language, and—on one thrilling and insecure occasion—he taught me how to drive a moto through the mountains.

Over those three short and long years of working together, Evens laughed, cried, danced, played lots of cards, hung off the backs of many a Toyota, helped clean the water flow out of wells, and became dear to every person who ever traveled with us. He was a vibrant example of the beauty and the best that Haiti has to offer, and I'm thankful that so many people across the political and theological spectrum who accompanied us to the island had the chance to link their lives to his.

Fifteen years later, when the Haitian immigrant diaspora was coming under threat of violence due to the dangerous rise of partisan rhetoric, Evens was living and working in Oregon. His wife and the mother of his four young children, who had generously stuffed me with fried plantain from her modest kitchen table, had passed suddenly years before. His new bride and their blended family of seven now resided in the Dominican Republic, where they'd escaped the more recent onslaught of gang violence erupting through their home country. When he and I reconnected, he was in year three of trying to go through all the correct, tedious, and impossibly expensive channels of the asylum-seeker process in order to be reunited with them.

When he asked our teams to support and share his fundraising efforts, it felt like an opportunity to not only repay him for all his love and care but also a chance to resist the limiting and harmful portrayal of (especially Haitian) refugees and migrants by the media. What I expected was quick generosity from former travelers largely aligned with immigrant-welcoming politics like mine. What I hadn't expected was name after name on the donor leaderboard to be those of folks who will often vote differently than I will, all because they'd loved him or loved someone who loved him.

Stories do what sound bites could never. Curiosity about a country and its people—Evens's and mine—had connected us past politics and through time, making room for relationships to transcend rhetoric and reminding me that weaponized generalizations (on all sides) should get so much less time on the microphone than curious consideration.

"If we have no peace," Mother Teresa is often attributed with saying, "it is because we have forgotten that we belong to each other."

If the world feels like it could use a little more peace—and it does—then maybe we must remember that we belong to each other. Getting curious, despite and especially because of how it leads us to vulnerability, might just make that possible.

***

Psychotherapist Esther Perel, renowned for her work in human relationships, once said that "most of us will have two or three marriages in this life. And if we're lucky, they're with the same person." I think it's fair to say that at a certain point in time, my husband Luke and I were nearing the end of our first.

Domestic life and parenting pressures could have stretched thin our connection on their own, as the rote routine of washing pants and paying bills and managing tantrums is wont to do. Having added a pandemic shutdown, years of infertility, owning a small business, and undiagnosed or unmedicated chronic conditions and neurodivergence, I woke one day wondering quietly, terrifyingly taboo sentences like, *Are we going to make it?* If a brave and vulnerable friend (or stranger) dares to speak such questions in my presence now, as if they're the first person ever to consider them, I am quick to say, "Oh, you're not talking to anyone here who hasn't asked the same thing." Life has an incredible propensity for rupture. Not everything lasts, and not everything needs to. But somewhere within me was the low rumble of our vows and a willingness, I could sense, in us both to explore repair.

When the clergyperson who married us spoke over our joined hands and into the crowd of overheated and sun-soaked wedding guests, he said, "Over the years, you will not grow in your commitment. You'll grow in the understanding of your commitment." I couldn't have possibly comprehended the depth of that statement at the time (nor fully now), but I understood enough to know that he was trying to convey how expecting, sometimes in vain, a promise to grow is different from exploring a promise that can hold growth. It's been one of the most precious foundational values anyone could have gifted us. Still, if I could go back to that moment and press for a slight edit, I would ask that he add, "You'll grow in the understanding of your commitment by staying curious."

I remember a night when we were both twenty-three and not officially dating yet when Luke came over to the apartment I shared with two other women to "fix our washing machine." As roommates and friends began to file out of the house to attend their various Friday night activities, he and I opted to hang back and talk. I can still see his six-foot-two, lanky frame extending the length of that thrifted futon as I sat adjacent on the other couch, volleying questions and wit. And I remember it feeling like I was unpacking an old cedar chest or excavating a dig site. He was an endless treasure to uncover, new and novel.

We talked about our grandmothers and our vices, our most embarrassing childhood memories, and the different versions of ourselves we'd shown the world and held most private. We shared music suggestions and doubts, travel horrors and hopes. At one point, he wiped tears away without reservation, and I knew this was someone not afraid of feeling. I felt the learning of him was inexhaustible.

Then one day, many, many years and jobs and changes later, I guess I'd subconsciously decided that it wasn't. I knew what there was to know, I'd seen what there'd been to see. I could predict the patterns and reactions in the same way that I could predict how our child's bedtime routine would go and what the weekend's Netflix shows would be.

In the timeless and quirky movie *When Harry Met Sally*, there is a scene where the main characters (whose friendship had just crossed a line into complicated) have both called their best friends, who are also in a relationship and together at the time, talking on two different phones. There is a woven chaos of hilarity as all four go in and out of talking on multiple lines about the same misfortune of dating. When the other couple hangs up their phones, the woman Marie says about dating to the man Jess: "Tell me I'll never have to be out there again."

"You'll never have to be out there again," Jess assures before the scene ends.

There's something universally relieving about the sentiment. Predictability and routine ensure stability, which any childcare professional will tell you should not be underestimated in value. Security is a gift. But for us, masked by and intertwined with the losses and stresses of life over an extended period of time, security had come at the cost of connection. Once I could identify the reality enough to find language for it, I thought surely life can't be as cruel as to make it one for one.

For erotically intelligent couples, Esther Perel says in her book *Mating in Captivity*, "love is a vessel that contains both security and adventure, and commitment offers one of the great luxuries of life: time. Marriage is not the end of romance, it is the beginning. They know that they have years in which to deepen their connection, to experiment, to regress, and even to fail. They see their relationship as something alive and ongoing, not a fait accompli. It's a story that they are writing together, one with many chapters, and neither partner knows how it will end. There's always a place they haven't gone yet, always something about the other still to be discovered."

There's always a place they haven't gone yet. I had begun my deep dive into curiosity at the point of reading this book for the first time, so I was exploring curiosity's power and properties, such as how it activates awe, infuses meaning, and is, maybe more than most things are, accessible. There was grace in remembering that we hadn't even begun to arrive at the end of us, and if humans are universes unto themselves (and we are), there was so much left to uncover, explore, muse on, play with, share, and ask. Curiosity about who we had and could become, alongside curiosity about our rhythms and brains and bodies that had contributed to who we'd been, could be the digestible next step to reconnection. In many ways, it has been.

I check in with a text thread of four women almost every day. All of them are lifelines, and one of them is a licensed therapist, which I can highly recommend having on tap. Over and over and over again, she reminds us (especially when we are sharing from the throes and woes of parenting and partnering) that perfection is overrated and honestly not helpful for raising whole and healthy humans. She'll note that it is better for a child to witness the ability and willingness to repair after rupture than for there to never have been a rupture at all. They're little humans in fact, she will remind, who will without a doubt cause and experience ruptures of their own throughout their lives. They need to know that reconnecting is possible after wounding and that we are better for both having happened.

You might even say that resurrection is possible after dying and that we are better for both having happened.

To practice the kind of curiosity that leads to vulnerability that leads to connection (or reconnection) is to bet on resurrection. I've known things that have lived again.

Reflection Prompts

Has rote routine or the stresses and losses of life caused you to categorize a relationship as predictable and exhausted, even if subconsciously? How might you practice curiosity to infuse novelty and remember there is always more to be discovered?

How have you witnessed survival-of-the-fittest at play? How have you witnessed survival-of-the-vulnerable or the connected at play?

Share your thoughts and experiences relating to rupture and repair.

How has communion been meaningful to you? What does it inspire in your life with your neighbors?

Nine

Curiosity Catalyzes Creativity

Everyone was filled with awe at the many wonders . . .
(Acts 2:43)

Right now, tucked into a corner shelf of a United Methodist Church basement, rests a stack of greeting cards made from collages of various pieces created through the community arts non-profit founded and supported by its congregation. In small, handwritten letters that appear between deep blues and crisp oranges are the words: "Less fear, more creativity." I can remember when one of the program's teachers and I, its director at the time, printed and folded those cards to send to neighbors and students in swift preparation to go into what we'd been told would be a two-week lockdown for something that was then being called the coronavirus. Scrambling for supplies and a plan before the church shut its doors added to the general societal sentiment that more fear was understandable, and creativity felt like luxury at best.

"You know, I had an art instructor who said I wasn't talented enough to be creative," the teacher who was helping me frantically organize said, as she pressed and stacked papers. "But I think what she meant was that I wouldn't be a good mimic, which is different than being creative. I didn't excel at copying her, but over the years, what I learned about myself is that I'm really curious, which helps me excel at using whatever I have to make something new and beautiful."

Taken out of my preoccupation with our task by her story, I stared, fist under my chin, and said, "It feels a little pie in the sky to hope that these cards might encourage some of that kind of curiosity over anxiety out there, but I guess we have to figure out how to make this all work for however long we have to."

"Ah," she smiled, "We're creatives. Finding a way to make it work is what we're good at."

Fortyish years before, the church in which we worked was given the opportunity to respond to its changing neighborhood dynamics by following money and safety to the south of town. Like the fear permeating the air during early lockdown days, the move to many would have been understandable, especially given the decline of pew participation and offering-plate giving—a downward trend that wasn't likely to end soon. Few would have blamed them for leaving. Still, they didn't.

Instead, the congregation voted not only to stay put and stay curious about the surrounding community and its shifts, but also to ask good questions and make good investments toward its most prevalent needs. With food insecurity and dropout rates swelling in the thirty-block area where a high percentage of the city's artists resided, the church made big moves with established partners to turn its basement into a food pantry, GED program, and community arts nonprofit. Long before congregations with the added cushion of neighborhood privilege began needing to ask questions about, and grasp alternatives for, diversified funding sources, multiuse building spaces, and creative community engagement, these folks were following the trial-and-error method of experimenting with a changing church. I was lucky enough to spend five years as the church's arts nonprofit director and learn from the resurrective power of playing with possibilities amid paradigm shifts.

I recall a particularly emotionally heavy week at work following the airing of footage captured at the disturbing and dangerous white supremacist Unite the Right rally in Charlottesville. It was my Tuesday to offer the chapel devotion at our staff meeting, and it felt important to explore together, following such rippling social anxiety, how curiosity might evoke our creativity and how creativity might evoke our hope.

"Are you with us or are you not? Are you faithful or are you not? Are you intelligent and loving or are you not?" I began. "These are the types of camp lines being drawn and enforced in our world right now, both politically and communally, but also denominationally, as we anticipate the plausible big and consequential changes for United Methodism in our near future."

I continued, "Our lives are saturated with more news of abundant tragedy and rapid innovation than any other century before ours thought possible *in this way*. And as earth stares down the barrel of extinction, our political pendulum-swing widens, and the institutional church fights the whispers and realities of disintegration. For many, it feels like chaos. For many, chaos is best combated with control.

"One form of such control is dualism, the reality of dividing something into two opposing states. In a dualistic world, we can contrive an ideology where we feel safer because we have defined who is the enemy and who is the friend, who is right and who is wrong, or who goes to heaven and who goes to hell. These categories contribute to our lives a (false) sense of security and power. Because, well, if we know who is bad, we can be good. And if we are good, we can have hope when we are scared.

"The problem is of course this: The world—humans, politics, faith, art, and so on—is far too complex to be pigeonholed into two categories. Furthermore, minds rarely change simply because someone has drawn a line and berated the opposing side long enough to convince them to hop over. I think I've never seen it happen. Like simple Sunday school answers, retaliatory violence, and Facebook fighting, feeding the machine of two-ways is an easy and unproductive route to take for multidimensional and creative people. I'll say it: Binaries are boring. They're certainly not the final fruit of the curious."

I then gave each in the group gathered a sheet of paper with a geometric shape of a quilt square printed onto it and a pack of colored pencils.

"I am going to now read off a list of hot, opposing topics and assign a color to each side," I warned. "You're then to pick a shape to color based on your beliefs and ideologies. If you fall somewhere along the spectrum, use both. If you are undecided or fall outside of the spectrum, choose a different color."

And all God's peacemakers said, "I'm sweating."

Republican, red. Democrat, blue.
Pro-life, purple. Pro-choice, orange.
Full LGBTQ+ church inclusion, brown. Limited inclusion, green.

The list went on.

"Now, you're each going to color the rest of your page based on aspects of your own special personalities and experiences. Take some time to make sure that there are shapes and colors representing things like your childhood, your passions, your trauma, your achievements, your interests, your loved ones, your fears, and your dreams," I said.

After a few minutes, I harvested the finished squares, shuffled them about like UNO cards, and hung them on a clothesline set up at the front of the room. It looked like a kaleidoscope.

"We are not altogether different people here," I remarked. "In this particular room, we're Americans. We live in Shreveport. We serve the same community. We know what a king cake is. Yet, we can see just by looking at this display that it would be impossible to separate us into two camps accurately. Each person brings too much to the table to be written off simply because of one color of one tiny shape.

"Every single person on planet Earth brings too much to the table to be written off simply because of one thought about one thing. So? How do we move out of two-way-only thinking? How do we encourage an alternative?" I prompted.

"Though I've considered the facts, I still find myself compelled by Jesus who was always subverting the narrative of 'friend or foe' by saying 'foe is friend.' 'Life or death?' Well, 'death leads to life.' 'Kingdom here or kingdom there?' *Yes*. Using mostly creative and confusing parables, Jesus found a way to disarm the this-or-that attacks of his day.

"'Who is right and who is wrong, God?' And God tells a story that evokes curiosity, catalyzes creativity, and challenges all sorts of listening ears.

"Over and over again," I began to wrap up the devotion, "God illustrates for us how to create opportunity for more imagination, stories, and questions than answers and judgment. Parables allow people to find themselves within the character that they most relate to in a moment, meaning we don't ever have to be anywhere we're not in order for God to speak to us. I suspect it is also so with our neighbors. Today, I may relate to the inn keeper in the story of the

Good Samaritan. Next year, maybe the wounded roadside man. Most days, I am the lawyer in the audience provoking Jesus to tell me the way to eternal life and getting miffed when he launches into *another* tale.

"Without curious imagination that leads to creativity, we brace ourselves for divine punishment or reward, while God floods the world with grace and the sun rises on both good and evil. Without curious imagination, we either argue violently or we cower in passivity, while the spirit prompts us to craft parables that appeal to the *imago Dei* in another. Without curious imagination, we compulsively categorize things as sacred or profane while Jesus holds up the very normal wine and bread and says, 'This is my body.'

"And while our feeds and screens, dinner tables, and pulpits shout *this life vs. eternity!— traditional vs. progressive! obedient vs. inclusive! innocent vs. criminal! right vs. wrong!*—it is worth creatively considering what actually relates to a life or changes a mind. Things like narratives, small steps, friendships across lines, stories of hope, content that evokes empathy, movement that shifts pain, humor and celebration, communion and confession. Curious, third-way creativity is about the veil-tearing, enemy-loving, sea-parting, tomb-emptying, early church-sharing, ex nihilo-creating, cheek-turning, land-healing, imaginative living into which we've been called and for which we've been equipped. But like any art, it must be surrendered to and practiced, embraced with vulnerability and forgiveness, and given room to contain multitudes all at once.

"The kingdom of God is always on the other side of the fences we construct," I concluded. "Curious, creative living is the holy mischief that wells up in our chests and asks if we're ready to hop said fence and paint a mural on the other side, or better yet, turn it over entirely to create a table for all."

I pulled the paper squares from the line, trimmed their edges, and placed them into rows of four. "A polychromatic, complex, and quilted wonder. And aren't we, though?"

***

When I hear people self-diagnose as not being creative, I'm quick to say it's hogwash. I don't believe there's a Creator-created human alive that doesn't share the DNA of co-creation. Do I think that the ways in which we've defined creativity are limiting? One thousand percent. But it would be very creative of us indeed to not relinquish our definitions to the monopoly, but to reclaim them in more inclusive ways, would it not?

Storytellers—whether they write books, share sermons, or lean over gas station counters in their overalls repeating the same tall tale—are creative. They're curious about connection.

Problem-solvers—whether they model emotional regulation and healthy conflict, rewire houses, or research for diagnoses—are creative. They're curious about solutions.

History-markers—whether they record with film, hold the traditions of a faith community, or collect the newspaper clippings of their grandkids—are creative. They're curious about who we've been and will be.

Innovators—whether they are experimenting with new ministries, designing prototypes for alternative energy, or illustrating simple animations for their three-year-olds—are creative. They're curious about possibility.

Prophets—whether they are naming the universally specific through poetry or liturgy, asking questions about the prison system, or looking around the room for who isn't there—are creative. They're curious about what's real.

Motivators—whether they work with youth, counsel young adults in their career choices, or seek God's vision for a specific community—are creative. They're curious about potential.

Reminders—whether they're telling you that you're needed, so keep going, guiding you through your own body's breathing, or naming where grace has shown up—are creative. They're curious about what's true.

Troublemakers (some of my favorite makers)—whether they're asking why things are done the way they're done, coloring outside of the lines, or meddling with new paths and new mediums—are creative. They're curious about what's not yet been said or seen.

An exhaustive list of curiosity-catalyzed creativity would fill a whole book in and of itself, but maybe it's sufficient to say *that creativity is the intrinsic human longing and ability to make a way*. This manifests in puzzle-solving, conflict resolution, poetry, systems, self-awareness and expression, gardening, marches, watercolors, spatial design, communications, healing, stitching, organizing, capturing stories, inciting hope and humor, and redirecting through limitations, among other things. A creative person is someone who recognizes within themselves the agency to contribute and cause; they recognize within themselves the invitation to join with a divine creator and other creative beings in an ongoing and unfolding narrative of hope.

And truly? We don't get where we need to go without them, without *us*. Here's a story of such curiously creative and interconnected way-making.

It was the year 1523, and a Benedictine nun named Katharina was a prisoner to her own life and faith. Though alternative options for the monastic seemed nonexistent, she, who had lived the convent life since her father first sent her away at age five, grew increasingly dissatisfied with her cloistered existence. Primarily to thank for this evolving reality was the explosion of public literature around the time, exposing her to alternative experiences and truths that she had not yet considered.

A little over a century before, a baby was born in Germany amid class wars to a wealthy father of the patrician class and a peasant mother. With hunger riots and election disputes plaguing the area, the child's family was forced to relocate multiple times for safety reasons, undoubtedly exposing the young boy to the harsh realities of hierarchy dynamics from an early age. With his mother's lower status likely resulting in his inability to succeed his father, a disillusionment with high society may have formed and added to his propensity to experiment outside of the box—a frowned-upon quality in a political-religious culture so dependent on the status quo.

Meanwhile, Roman Catholicism had wielded all control and funds for hundreds of years, with few changes and change agents to challenge the seemingly untouchable institution. With worship services offered in Latin only, while Bibles were relegated to (primarily male, celibate, literate) priests and monastics, exclusion of the poor and restriction to only the elite and educated had become the name of the game. Certificates of indulgences were sold and bartered to atone for sins, and spiritual authority was held solely by the pope and those who represented him. The church, once built on the unmatchable gift and unbridled grace of Jesus, had become synonymous with power, in bed with politics, exclusive, and restrictive. Sound familiar?

Not much is known about the German boy with the mixed-class parents during his youth and young adulthood. But around age forty, he would make a way that mattered, becoming a name that reverberated through the centuries. Johannes Gutenberg would go on to invent the movable-type printing press, which enabled faster printing, made restricted literature (like the Bible) available en masse, and incited the information revolution, which would make its way eventually to a convent in Nimbschen.

Years later, Katharina would absorb a piece of literature that flipped her world upside down in an instant. Once home to her lifestyle and ministry, her convent would become her jail, and she, alongside others who had read the same work, would grow eager to escape. Desperately, Katharina wrote to the author by whom she had been so moved and begged for help. The writer—arguably one of the most curious and creative way-makers in history— soon conspired with a merchant who often did business with the convent to smuggle several nuns off the property in empty barrels and assist them in beginning new lives outside of the confines of controlling ministry.

Katharina went on to marry the author of the life-changing work, run the day-to-day operations of their household, brew her own beer to sell to support their ministry, and help in the formulation and defense of her husband's movement. She became a force and a partner in what would later be known as the Great Reformation as the wife to Martin Luther, with whom she changed the course of church history as curious, creative mischief-makers in a significant paradigm shift of our faith story.

***

In nonprofit studies, Thomas Kuhn's theory of scientific revolutions is referenced frequently to describe and understand shifts like Luther's revolution. Kuhn explained how we begin with what we know at the time to be "normal science," which is standard puzzle-solving activities set within the current reigning paradigm. But then, an anomaly arises "when a puzzle, considered as important or essential in some way, cannot be solved." In the beginning, this anomaly can be written off as novelty, until it can't (either because it has gained attention or multiplied), which then becomes known as *crisis*. During crises, "new methods and approaches are permitted, since the older ones have proved incapable of rising to the task at hand (solving the anomaly).

Views and procedures previously considered heretical are temporarily permitted, in the hope of cracking the anomaly." Eventually, this leads to what we call a *paradigm shift*.

First, the norm.

Then, one anomaly.

Then, multiple anomalies, which we call chaos/crisis.

Which necessitates a revolution (led by the curious).

Which leads to a paradigm shift.

The people I have most often seen be quick to recognize opportunity and abundance during the chaos/crisis phase, rather than seeing it as an emergency or ending, are the curious creatives. These are the folks whose imaginations can conceive that life follows death, that making follows madness, and that possibility follows problems, and who don't fear those things. These people not only recognize that necessity is the mother of invention, but they know that curiosity may just be her womb.

In 2008, Phyllis Tickle cast the North American church as participating in "an every-500-hundred-years rummage sale"—a predictable cultural and religious cycle stretching back in various places over millennia. Tickle identified former 500-year rummage sales "as The Great Reformation (October 31, 1517), The Great Schism (1054—Greek Orthodox and Roman Catholic), the leadership and influence of Gregory the Great (540–590—following the fall of Rome and start of the Dark Ages), and the Crucifixion of Christ, which led to the birth of the Church at Pentecost." She also noted, astutely and long before many of her peers, that around five hundred years after the printing press launched us into the Great Reformation, another paradigm shift in information access (namely the creation of the World Wide Web) would usher in the start of a new rummage sale for both society and the church.

As the focus groups and strategic planning committees of Western churches continue to fret about church attendance and overcorrect with programming changes, the late Tickle's teachings call out: We are not becoming extinct as much as we are changing.

This is resurrection talk for resurrection people—creativity for the curious—if and as the church allows it to be; it's a season of purging, not perishing; experimenting, not expiring; and redefining, not defying, what it means to be Christian in this world.

New manifestations of following Jesus have emerged over the last several decades, pushing and crossing traditional lines with critical thinking, inventive imagination, and a resolve to take the words of Jesus literally. Tickle explored some of them in her book *The Great Emergence*. Missional communities, intentional communities, New Monastic communities, emergent communities, and dozens more have formed around values that vary in focus and function, but all have a common thread of loving God and loving neighbor at their center. Not only have such experiments taken shape, tried, failed, and tried again, but the "old institutions" have also entered a season of reworking necessitated by such an unavoidable paradigm shift. This was to be expected, Tickle said, as it happened five hundred years ago as well, when Catholicism didn't cease to exist with the formation of Protestantism, but rather reformed. Before her death, Tickle told us to anticipate both new manifestations of and reformations within our faith communities.

Whether brand new or reimagined, a running question fuels this development across the board: How are we, today, to be humans who follow Jesus? What does the way of the church look like in this age?

For two decades, I have wrestled and played with this question, both as a staff member of multiple (funding-struggling) faith organizations and as a founder and member of a short-lived New Monastic

Intentional Community. When I took all of my eggs out of the deteriorating "institutional church" basket in my twenties, and moved them over to be cradled by the still infant-like understanding of New Monasticism, I found that the wine skins were not yet ready to hold the weight of my eager need to discover or build "the new thing." I was desperate to find or make something concrete and established, while the very nature of the paradigm shift was—and is still—just that: shifting. Now that I spend most of my time in the dreaming circles of the reforming "old institution," I recognize that everyone's asking the same questions.

Where are the blueprints for all of this unprecedented change? Where does the money come from? What do the people want or need? What rules need changing? What stories need telling? How do and don't our practices fit within the society that surrounds us? Is this change sustainable? Where do we go from here?

My fifteen-year insistence on arriving quickly and decidedly at what and how the church needed to be *now* was the behavior of someone who does not recognize our collective calling to be the tension-dwellers rather than problem-solvers of this time. To be the kind of curious creators who "make prototypes, not presentations," as Reverends Matt Rawle and Rachel Billups are known to say on their curiosity-focused podcast *In the Sandbox.*

Phyllis Tickle predicted that it would take us—as it has taken others in the 500, 1,000, and 1,500 years before us—a hundred years to shake it all out once more, to find a new normal as humans, as Christians, and as people who are relearning how to love and recognize the image of God in one another. And if this is true, then we are still merely at the beginning of this epoch. We are in the "chaos" phase that every artist knows well, where the supplies are strewn about and the inspiration that is to be our painting's subject has yet to be fully grasped. To me, there is hope in this reminder—hope that maybe we have been created to live in the muddled period of *becoming*, committing ourselves to trial and error. It seems we have been offered the unique opportunity to experiment with several ways of existing, rather than finding, fossilizing, and marketing *the* way in our lifetime.

In this understanding, those disheartened by the continuous struggle of the church, or anything it's creating or recreating, to once again find its stride may embrace the reminder of persistence and the joy of curiously, creatively *playing with* all that is around us and within us to see what sticks and what doesn't. We are in the in-between; we may be here for a while. And we may have been specifically created and positioned as creators for this season of growth and change as Christ's body. Moses knew his people would land in a place he would never see, but he led them out of where they'd once been and set them on a long, tedious, creativity- and mistake-filled path of working it out. It may be that this is our story as well.

Might we, as mischief-making, creative, and curious tension-dwellers, commit to continuing to try and fail, sift and start over, and dream and hope, despite the odds that swirl around us? Might we commit to the becoming, even if we will never see the fullness of the being? Might we recognize how special this time in church history, and our participation in it, truly is?

***

"When the day of Pentecost came," it says in Acts 2, "they were all together in one place. Suddenly a sound like the blowing of a violent wind came from heaven and filled the whole house where they were sitting. They saw what seemed to be tongues of fire that separated and came to rest on each of them. All of them were filled with the Holy Spirit and began to speak in other tongues as the Spirit enabled them. Now there were staying in Jerusalem, God-fearing Jews from every nation under heaven. When they heard this sound, a crowd came together in bewilderment, because each one heard their own language being spoken. Utterly amazed, they asked: 'Aren't all these who are speaking Galileans? Then how is it that each of us hears them in our native language?'"

For so many reasons, I am fascinated by the story of the birth of the church at Pentecost, especially as it pertains to curiosity and creativity. Here in the context of Acts, we find a group of people who are in an interesting point of their timeline. Isolated, the story is compelling and mysterious—the spirit of God storms in and fills place and people, dancing like flames and conjuring drunken-like behavior that catalyzes a massive movement, affecting us all. Understood within the larger framework, we can notice even more at play.

A mere few weeks before this takes place, Jesus broke the bread and poured the wine for friends who would soon hide, lie, betray, grieve, and doubt him. Sacramentally, he offered grace, even and especially knowing that the mistakes would follow the meal, and the church would follow the mistakes.

After Jesus's death and resurrection and his reappearances to the disciples, the people were gathered, maybe for the Feast of Weeks (the fiftieth day after Passover, with *pente* meaning fifty). Or maybe they were gathered as people do once they've experienced such a shared trauma and hope. Here is when the spirit of God came upon them, adding to and redefining the faith narrative (as Pentecost would now be known as the marker of a new chapter for Christianity, not only a feast day for the Jews) and instigating otherwise impossible hearing and understanding between different people and tongues.

Of course, what happened next, once Peter delivered a message of interpretation and testimony for Jesus? The fellowship of believers seemingly exploded with creative collaboration and innovation, where communal connection was consistent and communal sharing eradicated the needs among them.

First the grace despite the imperfections (which is to say, grace).

Then, the power of the Holy Spirit to incite curiosity, redefine our narratives, and help us understand one another across our lines.

Followed by the creativity in community.

When my husband and I lived in and coordinated for a youth community house in an underresourced neighborhood, we met a local artist who wanted to work with the participating students to create a community mural on the house's back fence, next to the basketball hoop.

There was no way to know exactly what we would get once a dozen and a half eleven- to eighteen-year-olds donned black trash bags with arm and leg holes cut into them and simultaneously dunked their four-inch brushes into permanent outdoor paint. But there was grace in the invitation, despite the imperfections: The artist had created a paint-by-number-style outline of bungalow houses and ASL hands spelling out "love your neighbor" along the primed pickets. There was a curiosity among the students and leaders to play with the colors and with each other, to see what may lie within them and between them. This led to creativity that birthed community both interrelationally among the young makers, as well as visually in the gorgeous finished product—a vivid reminder to passersby that their neighborhood is filled with co-creators who know how to make a way.

Once the paint had dried, the artist came back through to clean up the edges and shade in the shapes, working all things together for the good. I took the children out back one cold and crisp March day to see the finished product. And after a collective gasp, one sophomore stood parallel to me and said softly and proudly, "Mrs. B, we made that."

There was no way to do it perfectly if we were going to do it together. There was no way to do it at all if we weren't going to do it curiously.

If artists required perfection for creativity, I'm not sure they'd ever get started. If the church required perfection for community, I'm not sure we'd ever have a chance. But like the grace that preceded the imperfections that preceded resurrection that preceded Pentecost that preceded the early Christian movement, curiosity precedes and leads to creativity and innovation in ways that make room for the mess. In ways that make it feel like the mess just may be a part of the whole thing.

How do we, together, get to the new and the next that we know is so needed and sense is on its way? How does a story get told, or a church reform, or a chapter get written? How does a conflict get navigated, or a problem get solved, or a mural get completed?

So rarely, with the insistence of immediate arrival. So rarely, with the expectation of certainty.

But with curiosity? With grace? With the grace of curiosity? I'd be willing to bet that with all new and next things that we've come to love and honor with great affection and gratitude, these were key pieces of their inception.

We may get filthy in the process. We may feel unmoored or uncertain (or be accused of drunkenness or heresy for contributing to revolutions). But nothing leads to creativity and community without the room to play, the room to try and fail and try again, the room to ruin a few clothes and disrupt a few systems, or the room to become who we're becoming while we're trying to get to where we're going.

If you're ever driving south past the corner of Gilbert and Dalzell near downtown Shreveport, you may see the remnants of a mural proudly proclaiming the words "We Love Highland." I hope it reminds you that your mimicking is not needed as much as your curiosity is invited to help you use what you have to make something new and beautiful for this world.

***

Reflection Prompts

Do you consider yourself a creative person? Why or why not? In an expansive understanding of creativity, how might you see yourself as creative?

When have you felt that perfection, certainty, or the status quo were restrictive to your imagination? When have you felt the room to play, try and fail, and follow curious creativity?

How have you sensed or witnessed the movement of a changing church? In what ways have you seen or dreamed of being creative with and for your faith community as you work out who you are becoming?

Consider a creative endeavor that you are interested in. What curious or collaborative first step can you start with?

Ten

Curiosity Rewilds Us

The bush was blazing, yet it was not consumed.
(Exodus 3:2)

In Exodus 3, the scripture says, "Moses was keeping the flock of his father-in-law Jethro, the priest of Midian; he led his flock beyond the wilderness, and came to Horeb, the mountain of God. There the angel of the Lord appeared to him in a flame of fire out of a bush; he looked, and the bush was blazing, yet it was not consumed. Then Moses said, 'I must turn aside and look at this great sight and see why the bush is not burned up.' When the Lord saw that he had turned aside to see, God called to him out of the bush, 'Moses, Moses!' And he said, 'Here I am.'"

There is a theme in the Bible—there is a theme in the Exodus story, God's story, and our stories—of homecoming and exodus . . . homecoming and exodus, cyclically. All throughout, we see this rhythm unfolding where God makes a home, and God's people leave it (or are forced to leave it, or invited to leave it), and then they go on a journey of remembering who they are and whose they are before the returning or homemaking anew. We see it in Genesis and

Exodus, we see it in all of the exile stories throughout the Old Testament; we see it in the prodigal son, and one lost sheep among the other ninety-nine, and even at the very end of Jesus's life, when he says *I am going to make a home for you*. Revelation is about homemaking, echoing Genesis, which is about homemaking and tells us right off the bat, and right at the end, that God's story starts and ends with home. It could be said of our personal experiences and the story of our collective and confusing faith that if we do not feel home yet, the story's not yet over.

Here in the Exodus story, Moses, who is the product of risk-taking women, was raised within the protection and privilege of pharaoh's house because his mother refused to let him be killed during the forced infanticide decreed as a means of population control among the Hebrew people. She set him in a basket as a baby along the Nile River, and the pharaoh's daughter found him and raised him as her own. Moses was brought up with an identity crisis. Was he Egyptian or Hebrew, or both, or something altogether different? And this identity crisis came fully to a head when he grew up and witnessed violence being inflicted by an Egyptian man on a Hebrew man. In his anger, he killed the Egyptian, hid the body, and fled for his life to Midian, where, mind you, he was still not home. But his displacement had a purpose. There was a reason why Moses was becoming so well-versed in a multitude of cultures and stories—God had work for him to do that he did not yet realize.

Then, one day, God spoke to a curious Moses from a bush out in the wild that burned but was not consumed. This is both one of my favorite parts of this story and descriptions of God because all the Hebrew people had known at this point was a power that consumed them. But this God could be powerful without having to destroy something, and that mattered. Moses's open curiosity about what *new thing* the wilderness fire might mean (a lovely nod to Pentecost) ushered in a new era.

I entered my relatively progressive—for our region—liberal arts school with a theology that could be best described as conservative-fundamental-light. With little understanding of privilege, few cross-cultural relationships, and great resonance with a martyrdom mentality within a kind of fragile faith that could slip away if one behaved or associated poorly, I joined the Christian Leadership Center, guarded and with heavy skepticism. I'd heard tales of their religious tolerance, which at the time (and this is hard to type) smacked of a diluted faith to me and, therefore, I entered my first few gatherings with natural withholding energy. By traveling out into what felt then like my wilderness, I was met with a grace I couldn't yet recognize, and it would be the thing that lasted the longest.

Over the weeks, then over the years, Christian students across the spectrums of theology, politics, economics, race, gender, ability, and sexuality would gather together in a gray-carpeted auditorium in the religious studies building. As curiosity was facilitated and practiced, space was made for the Spirit to meet each person where they were and for where they were going next. When I think about the approach of the leadership during that time, it feels very parabolic to me. As we've noted, throughout the gospels, people are constantly asking Jesus achingly universal and relatably human questions, and Jesus is always launching into a story, giving real Mr. Miyagi and Yoda vibes. But the older I get, the more I appreciate this brilliant narrative tactic, saturated with characters and layers, able to meet a variety of listeners as they are in that moment in time (and maybe as who they become next upon another hearing).

Stories (like the wilderness story) midwife our souls in ways that classroom lectures and debates and camps aren't equipped to do.

They make great space for *becoming*, like my campus ministry made great space for becoming.

Recently, I attended the fiftieth anniversary of this ministry, where five decades of alumni sat in the same auditorium, sharing stories of such room that had been made over the years as if it was the very DNA of the program from the beginning. I sat near someone who eighteen-year-old me had found difficult to understand and accept once upon a time. He was queer and Christian, a combination for which my brain had once held no box. And I'd been scared to know him, scared to get it wrong, scared to contribute to a storyline of harm as I'd defined harm at the time. But for all my fear, he remained curious about me. Curious about my thoughts, curious about my wrestling, curious about our similar upbringings, curious about collaborating in leadership. His curiosity trusted the Spirit's work in me in ways that didn't necessitate labeling me as *other* (which is quite merciful): It was a power that burned without having to destroy.

Years later, when I would share through memoir-writing a series of conversion experiences that had led to a far more progressive and inclusive theology, he asked for coffee and curiously wanted to know everything. His grace for my tears and apologies came as no surprise, as it had been there from the beginning. But I know that I know that I know that his willingness to make me a friend instead of an enemy made room for the Spirit to cultivate good fruit in wild places for me, eventually.

As someone who has experienced an emergency C-section, I know that sometimes fast and forceful change is what is necessary for lives to be saved. And sometimes, our required boundaries for safety and well-being do not allow us to get close enough to make friends of enemies. We can make room for that truth. But midwifing new life into the world *when it's ready*—through curiosity, and stories, and grace—whenever we can? There's a lot of beauty that can come from such a process, even if, and as, the gentleness seems counter-productive to the urgency.

Had someone not been curious about me *as I was* and *from where I sat*, I'm not sure there would have been as much room for God's spirit to move between and among us. I'm not sure we'd be the kind of friends we are today with the kind of bond we have. His openness and questions and care had been the merciful power that could transform but not destroy, like a burning bush or tongues of fire. My once certain and controlled theology had been invited all those years ago out into what felt like a desert where his curiosity evoked mine, eventually rewilding my domesticated story of faith and opening it up to new adventure. Such rewilding seeps into the soul of a person and makes it hard to unlearn that more beauty and becoming may lie across the boundary lines that we once set, and minded, to keep us safe.

***

To my delight, our nine-year-old recently started asking about kayaking, so I googled, "rentals near me" and found a gorgeous stretch of cypress-studded lakes and connecting channels for us to get our feet wet an hour away from our house. Once there, he sat in the front of a neon-green tandem boat, doing little more than kicking water back onto my husband, who was pulling both their weights. I scooted along beside them in a single kayak, remembering the full-body art of paddling.

"Are there alligators in these waters?" I'd asked the east Texas rental owner.

"Well of course there are," she said, "but you'll be lucky if you see one. We don't feed them, so that they don't associate us with food and the grandkids can keep swimming."

Feeling comically secure *enough* in that answer, we'd set out along the bayou. Immediately, my son settled into the open air as humans tend to settle into wild places. As we skated atop satin water, past thick mossy trunks beaded with baby turtles and freshwater mussel shells, woodpecker knocking echoed through the branches, making the sky feel domed. When we approached the "beach," which the map indicated was the halfway point, a million water bugs danced in synchronicity between our kayaks, looking like specks of magic that exist whether we're there to witness them or not. Our son clambered out of his boat's front and slopped around in the sandy shallows, while Luke and I drifted and breathed.

About fifteen minutes into playing, we decided to push out again in order to get to the "big lake" and back before our time was up. Right, left, right, left, we pushed to make minutes count. As I dug, I said a quick prayer, "Curiosity. Here."

Finishing a long, straight stretch with a bend ahead of us, all three of us looked at each other, half confused, half in wonder, as an unfamiliar series of sounds started to grow.

Phwup, phwup, phwup, followed by a skittering of splashes, followed by popping branches and (what could only be interpreted as) tiny dinosaur yelps. The uncertainty and volume of foreign sounds could have been enough to turn us around, I suppose; we were in unfed-alligator waters, for crying out loud. But *curiosity, here* pulled us forward.

As we rounded a jut-out of pines and entered the spaciousness of an alcove, our breath and paddles stopped. There, right in front of us, unfazed by our presence, was an entire kettle of turkey vultures bathing, roosting, communing, and thriving. We watched, wordlessly, as they majestically *phwupped* their wide-spanned wings into flight, circled, then landed heavily on swaying branches. New chicks and old birds walked in circles near the waterline, while a screeching several splashed in the bay.

Mesmerized, I considered all the life I was getting to witness in the wilderness through birds I'd once only associated with death—all the witnessing of life that curiosity, despite the unfamiliarity, had made possible, as had happened within the unlikely friendships of my college ministry. In the wilderness, I remembered that curious people encounter the *empowering* (not overpowering) Spirit and learn, or relearn, that God provides, good things grow in wild places, and belonging can often be found on the margins of what we once called home, making home even bigger and more inclusive than we ever once imagined possible.

***

Church people know how to be scared.

Those of us raised in or around evangelical Christian spaces have often spent many decades in the realm of risk-assessment pertaining to hell, piety, desire, and church attendance. Here, children are ever pointed to the waters of holy baptism—and reminded that hell awaits an unrepentant sinner's soul. Youth are praised for how well they're able to disconnect their idea of goodness from their bodies; young adults meet disapproval for any amount of deconstruction of faith that might affect their church attendance; and congregants are presented with statistics of emptying pews, withheld tithes, and the spiritual-not-religious whose growing numbers threaten the widely accepted definition of "church." Meanwhile, there is little space to question whether all the warnings are there simply to ensure that our church buildings can keep the lights on.

For many in the modern church, the constructs, language, and programming have been centered primarily on fear. And that fear has been centered on death. It is bizarre, is it not, that somehow the religion built upon life after death would devolve into an iteration so terrified of death? Yet, here we are: known for our fear of change, fear of eternal punishment, fear of being wrong, fear of allowing someone else to be wrong, fear of changing our minds, fear of losing comfort, fear of losing power, fear of other religions, fear of the nonbinary, fear of a faith separated from nationalism, fear of unweaponized vulnerability, and fear of dying.

We are afraid to die to self, to die too soon, to die forever. So often this fear looks like hate and feels like violence. I imagine that this is why we try to stay far away from whatever we consider the wilderness, because we've determined that life is more vulnerable there.

Our former neighbor, Ms. Sandy, was a retired preschool teacher who loved helping our kid be curious about the world around him. She stopped by our house a few years ago and gave our five-year-old at the time a dried cob of blue corn to plant, which he immediately did on top of the hill behind our house. We waited.

And we waited. And waited. And the thing never sprouted.

Until one day, months later, in a season when corn doesn't usually grow, it did. And we celebrated with stunned awe.

It would have been quite poetic, this waiting and eventual bursting-forth. But, of course, we forgot to tell the high school student who cut the grass on the hill that we had planted a random stalk of corn there. And one day, before I could even use its triumph for a sermon illustration, we came home to it Weed-wacked away, along with everything else.

It didn't come back.

Until it did. Eight feet away and three months later, in a part of the yard where, it was our best guess, the lawn equipment had flung it weeks before. And we got to watch it grow again with amazement and gratitude.

Until, of course, along with much of the rest of northwest Louisiana vegetation in the big and random freeze of that year, that resilient little corn stalk died, and our home mourned again. That is (still with me?), until midsummer, when we saw its long, spindly leaves pushing through the ground like the hero that it continued to prove to be.

This story makes me think about how a few years ago, a tornado ravaged the north end of Louisiana, where I live, and people three towns over lost everything—roofs, cars, jobs, a place to land. The drone footage that surfaced soon after was horrifying and incredibly sad. A year later, friends of ours returned to their home, finally able to move their family back in to attempt whatever it meant to start over. One day, in the back of their property, while cutting and piling broken logs and scattered limbs, they found—can you believe this—dozens and dozens of fresh squash growing between the debris, as if they had been planted there by the careful hands of a gardener. Yet, they'd never had a vegetable patch prior to the storm.

I love this story. Because—while I would be hesitant to flirt with the idea that God uses storms—it reminds me that life wants to happen (and is happening!) out in the wilderness and out in the deserts where we previously decided everything goes to die. It reminds me that the fruit of God's spirit is wild, uncontainable, and unwilling to be monopolized as the property of any one person, structure, or interpretation. It is alive and well today, coursing through our wreckage, reminding us that what we have is within us, and who we have has not left us.

I hope in this. And this hope is holding to the oldest tale ever told, a tale of gardens turned to mulch and seeds turned to roots. It's about not glossing over the realities and pain of dying, but it is about how we might both trust a death-like birth and navigate through it with the kind of imagination and curiosity that drives out fear. It's a hope that gives us permission to daydream, to be reformers in the beast's belly, or revolutionaries creating stuff that looks like heresy and feels like home; this hope enables us to craft new curricula, write new prayers, call God by names that disrupt oppression, and call the earth a sanctuary despite the warnings of those who need our money. It's a hope that gives permission to trust that the Spirit has ways and plans and connections and fruit that wants to be found, and that the curious might just be the ones to say, "I must turn aside and look at this great sight."

***

I took my son to see the movie *The Wild Robot* when it first came out and mortified him to the depths of his being with how much I wept through the whole thing. In addition to themes of unlikely family and unlikely friendships, climate change, and creation-resilience, there is a significant case to be made for the storyline of curiosity and its power to turn programmed things wild, and for that wildness to be relationally activating and existence-expanding.

In this animated film, set in the future, a service robot designed to help and accomplish tasks named Roz washes ashore on an unpopulated woodland island after a terrible storm causes her cargo ship to lose several of her models. Once briefly orienting herself, Roz sets out to do what she was wired to do: help, presumably humans. But since there aren't any, she quickly becomes an overeager (and terrifying) nuisance to any wild animal in her path. Along her journey, she becomes the caretaker and task-manager for an abandoned egg-turned-gosling whose well-being and growth go on to require an unprecedented amount of flexibility, evolution, openness, and reprograming on Roz's part, which ultimately leads to an almost humanity, wildness, wholeness, and love.

Without giving significant spoilers, two scenes took my breath away more notably than the others. The first follows a series of bumbling mishaps caused by this robot, who so desperately wishes to help but continues to do little more than disrupt or terrify the native species where she washed up. After countless fruitless attempts, Roz sits on the ground and engages in "learning mode," curiously paying attention, absorbing, and acclimating as several seasons pass. When Roz "wakes," her curiosity has given her the language of the animals and a better sense of her place in this new and changing world.

This leads her to adopt an orphan gosling, who she (and their fox enemy-turned-friend, Fink) must somehow teach to fly before winter sets in. The second breath-stealing moment for me came in the gorgeous scene where Brightbill the gosling is attempting flight for migration, and something in the preprogrammed robot Roz has flipped. In a very primal, deeply fierce moment of mothering, she takes off racing, plowing through the wilderness to the very edge of the highest cliff and lunging her metal body as far as possible while hanging onto the tallest jutting tree to get a last glimpse of the one who she now loves. The viewer knows that something that wasn't within her before is now writing the story—something that can best be described as human, relational, interconnected, real, raw, and wild.

There are so many more layers and commentaries to be explored about what was made possible by the relationships made possible by the wildness, in turn made possible by curiosity. But what was most beautiful to me was the profound story of who we can become, with unlikely characters in unlikely places, by engaging in a "learning mode" that has the power to activate or reactivate the wildness within us . . . and why that matters for the lengths that love can and will go.

To the businesswoman enslaved within the doldrums of deskwork and the status quo . . .
To the pastor who feels beholden to a domesticated version of faith . . .
To the young adult or immigrant or divorcee facing the daunting task of restarting . . .
To the person living the same day over and over and over again . . .
To the one who feels limited by your "programming" . . .

And the one who's starting to wonder if the wilderness holds more than the death that everyone warned them about . . .

To those who keep hurting with their helping and those having a hard time adjusting to change . . .
To the stuck and stagnant,
the curated and cultivated,
and the tamed . . .

The wilderness (that is to say, *all* of the unlikely places you thought life couldn't or wouldn't happen) may be calling. I hope you'll head into it curiously, whatever that means for you. I hope within it you'll find a power that does not consume but compels you to be and become all that you couldn't once imagine for the sake of the love that it may just make possible.

As Roz races—like a human, like a mother, like the embodiment of the bleeding-heart connections to everyone who has ever mattered to us—through the woods, Maren Morris's song "Kiss the Sky" swells in the background:

> *The unfamiliar road could be the same place you get lost and find yourself.*

I'm curious about your wilderness and who you may become there. The world needs the love made possible by it.

Reflection Prompts

Discuss or write about your posture and understanding of wilderness. Is it positive, negative, daunting, hopeful, or something else?

Have you ever had a friendship "across enemy lines"? What was your experience?

Let's dream for a minute. What might it mean for the Spirit to be found in the wilderness as a bush that burns but is not consumed for this day and context? What could homecoming and/or homemaking with God's people look like now if it grew up in wild places after the storm and wasn't beholden to any former structures or systems?

What parts of your life feel "preprogrammed" and in need of "rewilding"?

Eleven

Curiosity Activates Awe

Who is this? He commands even the wind and water.

(Mark 4:41)

Childhood wonder—do you remember?

I do, vividly, when I stop long enough to let it bubble to the top.

Among the small-swell sea of piney hills in north Louisiana, my grandparents, cousins, and immediate family lived within a three-mile triangle of each other. I have more memories of being outside than in, most of them colored with a level of freedom unfamiliar to my own child. So many Saturday and summer mornings, we kids would wake to pull on swimsuits, hunters' orange vests, and the oversized rubber boots that were piled up for communal use outside Mammaw and Pappaw's farmhouse. We'd pack baggies of pretzels, moon pies, and water bottles into mesh backpacks, then set out to explore the bottoms and bayous until dusk. Childhood wonder emanated from natural curiosity—that effortless openness to explore, discover, and be amazed by the world around us.

To the average passerby driving along the adjacent highways, this was just pastureland and ponds, stagnant and unstoried—like it can be to me when I drive past it now. But then, it was hay-bale castles with multiple stories climbing high into the old barn, acres of mystery and history with the surprises of large crystals and wild blackberries and unmarked graves and arrowheads, the wonder of what the dark water and dense tree lines held and hid, and a playground for creek-bed climbing, and mud-stew making, and feeling October's breeze sweep across sweaty brows. So many evenings, we'd return to the perimeter of the yard and hold out the barbed wire for each other to slip back through. Then we'd climb into the back of the old, empty dump truck or out the window of the second-floor guestroom to watch the oil spill of stars start to spread like we were wild children born in another century and not the '80s and '90s.

Metallic waves of minnows and mark-leaving thorns, gates to swing on and carcasses to stumble upon, mundane magic enmeshed with the rhythms of life and death that can't be concealed on farms: There was risk, and there was wonder. I miss how easy it was to know. I think, in many ways, I've been chasing it ever since.

Bike riding with arms outstretched, getting lost in books and corners, sinking calf-deep into rainstorm puddles, and turning everything into a prop for imagination—truck beds and dining room tables, leaves raked into floor plans, and bubbles so otherworldly they still don't seem real. Sunsets and paper dolls, sugared strawberries on red-brick porches, spiderwebs dream catching dew, peach juice dripping down to elbows. Cloud shapes and homemade water slides, falling asleep while grown-ups talked, raindrop races on road trips, the smell of old cedar chests. Bare feet, magnolia trees, homemade games, self-written and starred-in plays, and when the whole family would come outside to play a round of Horse, or shoot fireworks, or listen to the ice cream maker churn and groan while the cicadas sang of change.

In town, the old United Methodist Church held unused rooms and dusty crawl spaces that we'd squirm through and tell tales about while parents met in committee. Under the bleachers and inside blanket forts, we'd play with questions of what had been and what could be. And nothing felt quite as wonder-full as Christmas, and, maybe even more so, its anticipatory red carpet of Advent, with its Milky Way of lights and retold tales and songs and smells that suggested some things are special because they're brief and also because they come back around. Like life and death and resurrection.

That's probably why, at least in part, miscarrying for the first time during the holiday was so devastating . . . so awe-exiling.

After five years of trying for a second child, this was not the holiday season for which we had risked our hope. We had just found out she was a girl and were preparing to share the word *sister* with our people. I wrote this poem from the fetal position in our bed, following the first of many breath-stealing blood panels.

While the world awaits
the Christ child's birth, I'm waiting
for bleeding to start.

"Like contractions," the
nurse said. Except my womb is
a mortuary

for Christmas. I stare
at the ceiling fan, tissues
gripped. Mary's story

does not resonate
this year. Or last, or last. I
am Elizabeth,

Simeon, Anna.
And this body's the temple,
housing the waiting,

the dying, and the
indignant castle builders.
And mystery, too.

We found out a day
too late for Blue Christmas since
loss does not schedule.

Between stockings and
heating pads, our eight-year-old
deserves cheer still, right?

God, "Sister" was the
last gift I wanted returned.
But a gift. A gift

we'd so quickly made
room for in thought and words and
he called you August.

But now this Eve feels
like last May, which felt like the
last five long years when

yesterday felt like
a miracle we had let ourselves
make a new home in.

His tears caught up at
bedtime, and I soothed, "Someday."
"But how do you know?"

he pushed. And I don't.
Joni's "River" feels welcomed.
Could we skate away?

Advent has ended
by restarting. A thrill of
hope turned weary world.

Emmanuel, God
with us, God with us, here. If
nothing else, please be.

In that gray moment, awe felt impossibly distant, like a dream that was fading.

By the time our first miscarriage started, I was very familiar with Dacher Keltner's book, *Awe: The New Science of Everyday Wonder and How it Can Transform Your Life*, thanks to my therapist's suggestion. It became an unexpected lifeline when wonder seemed furthest from reach—when one might easily ask if awe ever really stood a chance given how obscenely fragile life can be. I'm certain it helped that Keltner writes from a place informed by pain.

He says of his brother's death, "With his passing, I felt *aweless*. And my companion in awe was no longer around to help me make sense of the vastest mystery I had encountered in my fifty-seven years of living. A loud voice called out: FIND AWE. Knowing of awe's many benefits, and that we can find it all around us, I went in search of awe. I took a moment each day to be open to the awe-inspiring around me. I sought out places of importance in the history of awe. I engaged in open-ended conversations with people I considered awe pioneers. I immersed myself as a newcomer in various wonders of life. These explorations led to personal experiences, memories, dreams, and insights that helped me make sense of losing my brother. They brought me to the conviction that awe is almost always nearby, and is a pathway to healing and growing in the face of the losses and traumas that are a part of life."

I went in search, he says. *I took a moment to be open . . . I sought out . . . engaged . . . considered.* To me, this sounds significantly like the discipline of curiosity, which faithfully enabled the resurfacing of wonder in Keltner, despite all odds.

"Awe," as Keltner defines it, "is the feeling of being in the presence of something vast that transcends your current understanding of the world." It's that which "expands our sense of self from feeling independent to feeling part of something larger."

The benefits of stimulating awe are remarkable, the science demonstrates. Keltner's team's research shows that those experiencing more awe and wonder in their worlds fare better against threats and unknowns and have greater joy, more connected community, and healthier lives; they are more likely to find the extraordinary in the ordinary, are more open to mystery, new ideas, and the virtues of others, are empowered to sacrifice and inspired toward generosity, have lowered chronic inflammation, and are likely to lead deeply rich spiritual lives.

Why does this matter, one might ask? "Because," he shares, "awe allows us to get outside of ourselves, and integrates us into larger patterns—of community, of nature, of ideas and cultural forms—that enable our very survival . . . wild awe awakens us" to the "ancient way of relating to the natural environment. And in this awakening, we find solutions to the inflaming crises of the times, from overstressed children to overheated rhetoric to our burning of fossil fuels. Wild awe returns us to a big idea: that we are a part of something much larger than the self, one member of many species in an interdependent, collaborating natural world."

This feels like such a crucial resource right now in a world where anxiety diagnoses soar, infighting and line-drawing run rampant, an inundation of urgency and trauma from our global access to information becomes relentless, and systems and patterns continue to perpetuate questions of *why any of it matters anyway*. We need awe more than ever. I think curiosity could be a key to unlocking it: one we'll likely realize—to our thrilling surprise—was in our pocket the whole time.

In a chicken-or-egg query, we could wonder what comes first: curiosity or awe. Keltner might say that we access awe through eight wonders (moral beauty, collective effervescence, nature, music, visual design, spirituality/religion, life and death, and epiphanies), and then that wonder-released awe leads to things like curiosity and openness. Based on my own lived experience (and maybe the order is trivial), I feel like those eight wonders are pregnant with awe when approached curiously—a practice and posture that might prove to be more accessible than the hope of stumbling upon wonder.

***

The relationship between curiosity and awe appears throughout scripture, perhaps most vividly in the moment when the disciples encounter something beyond their understanding amid tragedy. In Luke 8, it says, "One day he got into a boat with his disciples, and he said to them, 'Let us go across to the other side of the lake.' So they put out, and while they were sailing he fell asleep. A gale swept down on the lake, and the boat was filling with water, and they were in danger. They went to him and woke him up, shouting, 'Master, Master, we are perishing!' And he woke up and rebuked the wind and the raging waves; they ceased, and there was a calm. He said to them, 'Where is your faith?' They were afraid and amazed, and said to one another, 'Who then is this, that he commands even the winds and the water, and they obey him?'" The disciples could have said anything following Jesus's command to the sea and wind.

What took you so long?

Would you have let us drown had we not stirred you?

Do you care?

Instead, they are inundated with awe and filled with curiosity about who they've kept company with all this time.

On the religious website Patheos, writer David Roberts shares, "Though we might like it to be, this isn't a story, I don't think, about Jesus' ability to control the weather. He is bothered to perform the miracle and is annoyed, it seems, that his disciples even asked. This is a story, rather, about how little we believe God to be with us in the midst of an overwhelming storm. It's about how, deep down, maybe we don't really believe that a God-with-us is actually enough . . . I don't really think the miracle in this story is about Jesus calming the storm and taking control. The miracle in the story is that Jesus was with the disciples in the water-logged and weather-beaten boat, experiencing the same terrible storm, the same terrible waves, the same terrible danger. And that alone should have been enough. God's power isn't in the control of creation or of people, but in being in covenant relationship with them."

Who then is this, the curious and now awestruck disciples ask. That kind of realization of holy company, through hell and high water, regardless of the outcome, changes a person, and shifts their sense of connection and capacity, which, I believe, shifts their fear.

Who is this that is with us—though storms and addictions and wrecks and cancer remain possibilities? Whose presence and power can we find and refind in Keltner's moral beauty, collective effervescence, nature, music, visual design, spirituality/religion, life and death, and epiphanies? What awe does his company conjure, and what does that equip us with going forward?

How does that awe help us keep going when continuation feels unlikely? How might it remind us of one of the most healing truths available to us: that there's no place we can go that God has not been, or that God will not be?

What confidence and connection does trusting and seeking such awe offer us in a vulnerable world?

***

I am grateful to have borne witness to how even small acts of curiosity can reignite awe in unexpected moments throughout my life.

On the day of my grandad's memorial gathering, a fair barn was filled with friends and kinfolk and babies romping around in overalls. There were jugs of sweet tea and pans of fried fish, country music, and scanned photos. People we didn't know drove in. Five little oak trees lined the stage in memory of Pappaw on behalf of his grandchildren. They would be buried with his ashes in that good southern soil where we'd adventured with cousins among life and death and life again all those years ago. A few nights before, when his levels had begun dropping and his breathing became raspy, I wondered if it might make any difference to anyone if I took my guitar up to the nursing home. I was curious if he could hear, if he was in any way still present and aware, if it would make anyone uncomfortable or comforted to sing together as he made his way from one life to what we all hope is another. I shuffled past the crowded knees of my parents and grandmother and began to tune an underused instrument while more cousins and close friends squeezed in. With no other disclaimer, we began singing to the poorly plucked notes of "Blessed Assurance," "I'll Fly Away," and Sandra McCracken's "We Will Feast," the last of which happened to be the song I listened to on repeat as I tried to usher my infant firstborn out of the womb and into his new existence. How special it was to be a part of midwifing someone into their next life.

Timid curiosity birthed awe despite death.

A year after the almost life-claiming car wreck of my own brother and all the surgeries that followed, my parents, brother, husband, son, and I flew to Chicago for vacation. On top of our own shared trauma, subsequent EMDR therapy, and months of my brother being bed-bound while recovering, it was also 2019, and our country was fraught with election anxiety at the same time our family was navigating the recent passing of our patriarch. Getting away from the Louisiana heat and getting some deep-dish pizza would be a welcome change of scenery. Though Chicago taught me that there are places hard to hate in August (unlike southern states whose rising heat makes it impossible to be outside), I owed its baseball team little allegiance prior to our trip. Still—I supposed—I was curious to see how many of my high school statistician skills still lived in the back folds of my brain. RBI, 2B, HBP . . . it turned out, quite a few were locked away dormant, apparently waiting for Wrigley Field.

The Cubs won that day, thank God, seeing as how my devotion went from zero to gift-shop purchase of a ball cap in less than nine innings, but I remember almost nothing about the actual game. Rather—and I think I may never forget it—I recall vividly how something like epoxy poured over that random crowd and my family and me as we stood to sing the infamous ending of "Go, Cubs, Go"; it made me feel alive, connected, and thankful—and like I would take a bullet for anyone in that stadium. Different humans, otherwise not belonging to each other, were all having the same human experience, in which loss is inevitable but awe is discoverable. Same tune, same air, same beat, same team. Whoever they were and wherever they are now, however they vote or raise their children or deal with their storms and their demons, for a moment in time, same team. Which meant that it was possible.

Communal curiosity ushered in awe after loss and division.

A few weeks after our Christmas miscarriage, I had to travel south for work. My mom, who was worried about me, asked to join my road trip, but I was hesitant to say yes as a lonely eight-hour car ride sounded quite cathartic. *Could this be what I need?* I wondered, as I reluctantly pressed send on a compliant response text. A couple of days later, we headed for Baton Rouge. While driving, we talked about the early years of her marriage, when she and my dad lived near LSU. She told me stories I'd never heard and took me to restaurants that had outlived decades of changes. We decided, pretty spontaneously, to go to an LSU women's basketball game against South Carolina that night and the funeral of a beloved pastor in New Orleans the following morning. Both events represented loss, like the trip itself did for me, but both were so undeniably drenched with layers of rich connection, belonging, and "leaving everything we've got on the court," because—no matter what's at risk—it's worth it. We sang "Callin' Baton Rouge" at the tops of our lungs beside the student section, while the band led the pulse of the crowd. We sang "When the Saints Come Marching In" at the tops of our lungs while the grieving and celebrating made a second line to the funeral reception.

Open curiosity unleashed connective awe where unexpected.

In the months following, we would end up rounding the corner of the following Christmas and into another year of secondary infertility that included our second miscarriage. On top of deep grief and bodily pain, I could have felt only, and justifiably, bitter about the multiple teasers and trampolined expectations—bitter, numb, tender, and worn out. But it had been seasons since that conversation with my therapist in which she invited me to a journey of curiously refinding awe, and I now felt other things as well.

I felt proud of our resilience and invited into the peace of our reality. I felt grateful for the love and care and understanding that our people interjected into every gray corner we'd let them into since the ultrasound tech's tone had changed. I felt sad, but not despairing. Pressed, but not crushed.

I felt open to magic that is not contingent upon a painless life, open to communion with God and neighbor that does not require an absence of storms, open to awe that is bigger than endings.

Mostly, I felt curious about, and awestruck by, what my body knew, what she could do, how she could hold me, how she could love me like a mother—fiercely and steadily, though I'd flail and rage in misunderstanding, and faithfully and lovingly, though I'd accuse and reject amid the wind and the rain. A body like a mother, a mother like God. A God who was with us.

Through loss of little lives and big dreams, family traumas, and daily challenges—though the threat of grief and pain persists, and the wonder of childhood seems sometimes elusive because of what we now can't unknow—the magic of awe is all around us, activatable by the smallest amount of curiosity, its heartbeat betting on there being *more* here than what we know or see.

Awe lies waiting in raised and released butterflies, choirs and congregants singing a transcendent "May the Lord Bless You and Keep You," and rereading books about wizards and hobbits.

It's in birds who play in hurricane bands, helpers who show up after the storm, casseroles on doorsteps, kindness in drive-throughs, lights and stars and ball games and second lines.

It resides in resilient people and communities who believe in a better world enough to invest in it, and in singing with new strangers and old friends, singing with the dying, and singing with the living, the losing, and those who belong to each other when it's all said and done.

Awe lies in fireworks and mountain summits and rooftops that let you see the whole city, in Christmas ornaments wrapped in paper that say *August*, and in Chicago in the summer—in all the memories that not one thing can take away.

There are unavoidable reminders that life and loss can rob our very-needed awe, but curiosity can help us rediscover it, and the tools we need remain always at the ready. Awe is an invitation to adventure and play wherever you are and whenever you can, and when you see a spot of magic out in this often-mundane world, to follow it. Awe is also in Advent songs, of course, that come around again every December no matter what the year has held.

Long lay the world in sin and error pining
Til he appeared and the soul felt its worth.
A thrill of hope, the weary world rejoices
For yonder breaks, a new and glorious morn!

Emmanuel, God with us. God is with us, here. How wonder-full.

Reflection Prompts

What comes to mind when you think about the awe and wonder of childhood?

Have you ever experienced or witnessed loss or pain that makes existence feel impossible? If you have not, have you experienced fear of such an experience?

When is a time that awe has felt hard to come by? Where do you experience awe in your daily life currently?

Considering Dacher Keltner's eight wonders of the world (moral beauty, collective effervescence, nature, music, visual design, spirituality/religion, life and death, and epiphanies), where could you practice curiosity this week that might lead you to the activation of more awe?

Twelve

Curiosity Rewrites with Hope

Why do you look for the living among the dead?
(Luke 24:5)

Toward the end of the summer, during the part of July when it's best to wait 'til dusk to walk the dogs, my family went on a normal stroll around our normal route, sharing our normal questions and concerns about a normal week. Same old, same old, and maybe a little worse: The small business was in its umpteenth consecutive week of a dry spell, I had writer's block, there were quizzes to study for, the updates from loved ones had been distressing, and the news had been oppressive, as usual.

But as the sun started to head to bed and we made the turn to do the same, a tiny and sudden swell of light flashed on and off between the oak trees in front of us. We all gasped, stopped, and waited. "A . . . a firefly?" my son eventually whispered as we scanned the area to see if we'd collectively imagined it. Then it happened again, and again, and again, each time appearing in a part of the frame that we hadn't predicted, creating a beckoning breadcrumb path of magic to follow.

There aren't as many fireflies as there used to be, scientists say, so if you had a hunch that fewer abound, that's probably because you're paying attention. More than one cause is probable, but all causes point back to the loss of habitat as fireflies thrive in grassy settings with low light pollution. I'm quite mesmerized by these vanishing wonders for reasons that go beyond their heaven-come-to-earth, ground-level-starry-sky gift to us all. Fireflies (or lightning bugs, depending on where you were raised) are bioluminescent beetles that have a special organ in their abdomens that houses a substance called luciferin, which, mixed with the oxygen they breathe, creates a chemical reaction that produces the flashes of light that, when lucky, we get to witness. This light is known as "cold heat," since 100 percent of its energy is produced by the chemical reaction, and therefore the light doesn't produce heat like a flame would. With this cold heat, the bugs talk to one another.

I can't think about their cold heat without thinking about the bush that burned but was not consumed, or about curiosity's grace-like power to help us become *more than conquerors*, but ones in a place where we all arrive, and no one is destroyed. I can't help but muse on what it takes to cause that flash of light that enables their communication, like that curious head tilt that my counselor suggested for slowing reactions down. "At the very least," she had encouraged, "it will give you a chance to breathe and give goodness a chance to guide." In other words, a chance for my oxygen to give the light the opportunity to do the communicating—the light that burns but does not consume.

There isn't as much light-led communication happening around us these days, so, again, if you had a hunch that less abounds, that's probably because you're paying attention. I imagine loss of habitat has something to do with it; we've created spaces and narratives and faith communities that may interpret a curious pause as a nuisance or a luxury or a weakness instead of a strategy or a gift. But I do wonder what it could mean to create more spaces and narratives and faith communities that trust that curiosity might just rewrite even the most desperate and urgent story with hope . . . that curiosity might create ecosystems that invite the light and keep the conversation going.

When declaratives can communicate a full stop, curiosity suggests that the conversation continues. When the conversation continues, hope has a heartbeat. When hope has a heartbeat, resurrection is possible, even if it feels long in coming.

"On the first day of the week," it says in Luke 24, "very early in the morning, the women took the spices they had prepared and went to the tomb. They found the stone rolled away from the tomb, but when they entered, they did not find the body of the Lord Jesus. While they were wondering about this, suddenly, two men in clothes that gleamed like lightning stood beside them."

The traumatized and grieving followers had arrived to finalize the devastating story with dignity and closure. But where they expected a period, a question mark was offered. "In their fright," the passage continues, "the women bowed down with their faces to the ground, but the men said to them, 'Why do you look for the living among the dead?'"

We in our own lives would love to be looking for the living; but for many, everywhere we turn right now has the potential to feel like a tomb of dead and dying things, things for which we can do little more than visit and grieve. While our political landscapes feel dystopian and diversity goes on trial, migrants fear for their lives and those of their children. While mercy is mocked in the public square, genocide is a modern horror, and anything outside of the binary is criminalized, bullies continue amassing power and trauma piles up. Look for the living? Why? We've just seen the living crucified.

Recently one night, after our son had been asleep for a bit, my husband and I sat on the back porch near the trampoline where, last summer, we once wonder-hunted overlooking the bayou and the fireflies revealed themselves to us. He was sharing his concerns about the state of the world and how the threats in the day's news felt ever-encroaching into our daily lives. I listened, but only barely.

"You okay?" He asked. I'd been curiously thinking about whether I was, and why I probably wasn't, throughout most of the evening. I replied, "I spent most of the day combing through edits of my curiosity book—so many chapters were written through those months when I still thought that viable pregnancy and family expansion were in the cards for us. I can hear the hidden hope woven through." Our third miscarriage (and all the endings that it could and would mean) had happened a few weeks before.

"But," I continued, "When I ask myself what's going on within me, I feel I am simultaneously getting to know this new and deep grief while also experiencing a level of peace and presence in our actual lives (*likely due to a decrease in the self-discrepancy gap, or the real and wished-for selves coming together*) that I have not felt in a really long time. They're both profoundly there. And they both make me think that maybe life does come after all of this death, even and especially if that life is a more saturated version of the one we already have. I am sad, but I am curious about what could be ahead. The road looks different, this season looks liminal, but life does not look gray. I couldn't have always said that."

Our conversation that night reminded me how desperately we all need ways to hold both grief and hope, endings and beginnings, reality and possibility. This isn't just my journey—it's a collective need in a world where so many stories seem to be ending without resolution. We need help. We need something that can aid us in rewriting the stories that we feel are inevitable, out of our hands, and irredeemable. We need the grace of curiosity to shine its light where we least expect it can and say, "I'll take it from here. This is not the end."

Like with love, something appears inefficient about curiosity, as though we're taking the long way around to get where we need to go. And yet, all that we have explored about the grace of curiosity beckons: What if the sometimes-long way around *is* the way around? What if the curious way *is* the way of love? What if the question keeps the conversation going? What if the breath makes room for the light?

What if it matters who we're becoming together on our way to where we're going?

What if fear says we should get there as fast as possible, while curiosity offers that we could get there as whole as possible?

What if this is not my enemy?

What if I have something to learn from this moment? This person? This pain?

What if we can change our minds?

What if we have yet to arrive?

What if I need them? What if they need me?

What if there is still magic to be found?

What if there is still meaning to be made?

What if we can try again?

What if peace is available?

What if this is mystery, and mystery is adventure?

What if we could become the answer to our prayers?

What if the needle could move?

What if we have what we need?

What if awe can come after an impossible loss or amid overwhelming fear?

What if there's a way we could get there without destroying each other?

What if what looks like death is really rebirth?

What if my feelings and body and circumstances are communicating with me?

What if there is more here than what we can know right now?

What if the world is bigger?

What if I am a part of something longer, vaster, richer, better, and truer than I can imagine?

What if there's a story to be found or made?

What if life could have color again?

What if grace has gone before us?

What if we can extend that grace to the world?

What if God is here?

What if this is not the end?

When your worries take up too much of your own "portrait," I hope curiosity will help you find yourself somewhere where you can feel small and connected to the bigger story again. When your options seem limited to fight or flight, I hope curiosity disarms your default self and offers a third way. When life feels too fast, too fleeting, too meaningless, too isolated, I hope curiosity leads you to your pace, your purpose, and your people a little more over time. When shame's voice feels foundational, I hope curiosity lets the voice of goodness speak louder. When life and faith feel domesticated and dormant, I hope curiosity unlocks the wild creativity within you that the world so desperately needs. When you need awe to keep going, I hope curiosity reminds you how close and accessible it is, how ready it is to help you find it.

And when death feels final, I hope curiosity will help you wonder if life may be up around the corner even still. I hope you'll follow that curiosity one breadcrumb, and paused breath, and light flicker, and star gaze, and connection made at a time, for the sake of your wholeness and that of your neighbor and world. And I hope that you leave these pages holding curiosity not as a luxury or a hindrance but as a remarkable means of grace, irrefutable in value, and vital as a practice for the shared and available healing of us all.

What if another story—another world— is possible, one curious question at a time?

Reflection Prompts

What comes to mind when you think about "the long way around" of grace and curiosity?

Through what examples from Jesus's life, or your own life, have you witnessed this?

How has curiosity rewritten with hope? How might it rewrite with hope?

Create your own "what if" prayer.

Acknowledgments

As a person whose shadow self often gravitates toward certainty, I have depended on a ridiculous wealth of souls and settings to unlock the value of curiosity within me. This book is only possible because of people and places like Centenary College of Louisiana, the Christian Leadership Center and Rev. Betsy Eaves, Garrett Evangelical Theological Seminary, and my mentors and colleagues within the Louisiana Conference of the United Methodist Church and the United Methodist Foundation of Louisiana, who have all made room for every curious conversion and calling I have experienced in my life.

My parents named grace early on—and ever since—as utmost, which allowed me to recognize it when experienced most profoundly in curiosity. To name the friends who formed me, and the ones who keep me open, as invaluable to these pages would be an understatement. I especially want to take the chance here to thank Katherine and Maggie for musing on a bigger world with a younger me when it mattered, as well as Adam for trusting the longer arc of my story. I feel overwhelming gratitude for every doctor who spent time with me and every therapist who listened; in many ways and seasons, their curiosity saved my life.

Thank you, Lisa, my editor, and Broadleaf for being curious about a book on curiosity, for seeing it as timely and needed, and for guiding me with generous clarity and encouragement.

Luke and Bridger, your curiosity is hardwired and enchanting. I hope to be more like you when I grow up.

And for you, curious reader, I'm thankful for your openness and your time. The world is a lot, and it is often so hard to be human. You're here anyway, taking a chance on curiosity, on grace, as a precious gift and critical strategy for healing unto wholeness together. May it offer you a next step if and as you need one.

Notes

Introduction

xi ***"Come thou fount of every blessing":*** Robert Robinson, "Come, Thou Fount of Every Blessing" (written 1758), hymn first published in *A Collection of Hymns Used by the Church of Christ in Angel Alley Bishopsgate*, 1759.

xii ***"Curiosity is a fundamental Christian practice":*** *Igniting Imagination*, podcast, "Expanding Imagination with Amy Oden," TMF and Wesleyan Investive, December 16, 2021, https://ignitingimagination.org/podcast/expanding-imagination.

xiii ***"Prone to wonder, Lord I feel it":*** Robert Robinson, "Come, Thou Fount of Every Blessing."

Chapter One: Curiosity Is Accessible

2 ***humanity is and has been trending toward betterment and a more peaceful existence:*** Steven Pinker, *The Better Angels of Our Nature: Why Violence Has Declined* (New York: Penguin Books, 2023).

3 ***levels of depression and anxiety are far higher than a hundred years ago:*** Alex Kourt, *The Curiosity Gene: On the Origin of Humankind by Means of Intrinsic Motivation* (CreateSpace Independent Publishing, 2017), 149.

3 ***curiosity may just be the highly accessible, ever-present onramp to another way of being human:*** Todd Kashdan, Provoked (blog), accessed

January 30, 2025, https://toddkashdan.com; Lucy Caldwell, "Curiosity as an Antidote to Burnout," OMT Global, accessed January 30, 2025, https://www.omtglobal.com/curiosity-as-an-antidote-to-burnout.

3 ***pursuit of novel experiences, knowledge, and meaning in their mundane lives demonstrated more resilience:*** Eva Garrosa et al., "How Do Curiosity, Meaning in Life, and Search for Meaning Predict College Students' Daily Emotional Exhaustion and Engagement?," *Journal of Happiness Studies* 18, no. 1 (2017): 17–40, https://DOI:10.1007/s10902-016-9715-3.

3 ***shifting their "nervous systems from fight-or-flight to rest-and-digest":*** Duane Montrose, host, *The Addicted Mind*, podcast, "Episode 11: Beyond Recovery: Cultivating Curiosity for Emotional Wellness," March 21, 2024, https://theaddictedmind.com/tam-episode-11-beyond-recovery-cultivating-curiosity-for-emotional-wellness.

5 ***we have a basic need for awe wired into our brains and bodies:*** Dacher Keltner, *Awe: The New Science of Everyday Wonder and How It Can Transform Your Life* (New York: Penguin Press, 2023), xvi.

10 ***climbing in numbers of the "unaffiliated" since the early 90s:*** Pew Research Center, "How U.S. Religious Composition Has Changed in Recent Decades," September 13, 2022, https://www.pewresearch.org/religion/2022/09/13/how-u-s-religious-composition-has-changed-in-recent-decades/.

10 ***aware of the "rummage sale" decades in which we find ourselves:*** Phyllis Tickle, *The Great Emergence: How Christianity Is Changing and Why* (Grand Rapids: Baker Books, 2008), 14.

12 ***Passion is rare; curiosity is everyday:*** Elizabeth Gilbert, "One of the greatest quotes on creativity ever . . . ," blog entry on Elizabeth Gilbert's official website, posted February 8, 2014, https://www.elizabethgilbert.com/one-of-the-greatest-quotes-on-creativity-ever-i-am-a-big-advocate-for-the-purs/.

12 ***In these patches of joy, these stretches of sorrow, there's enough for today:*** "Enough," by Sara Groves, track 5 on *Floodplain*, Fair Trade/Colombia Records, 2015.

13 ***"Give us today our daily bread":*** Matthew 6:11 (NRSV).

Chapter Two: Curiosity Leads to Humility

15 ***Such diminishing/transcending opportunities go on to "orient the individual to the needs of others":*** Dacher Keltner, and Marianna Graziosi, "Awe: The New Science of Everyday Wonder and How It Can Transform Your Life," White paper, Greater Good Science Center, University of California, Berkeley, September 2018, https://ggsc.berkeley.edu/images/uploads/GGSC-JTF_White_Paper-Awe_FINAL.pdf.

17 ***"participants enjoying an expansive view also reported a greater sense of humility":*** Dacher Keltner, *Awe: The New Science of Everyday Wonder* (New York: Penguin Press, 2023), 33.

17 ***researchers have attributed perseverance to humility and humility to curiosity:*** Greater Good Science Center, "Introduction to Intellectual Humility Research," University of California, Berkeley, accessed January 30, 2025, https://ggsc.berkeley.edu/what_we_do/major_initiatives/intellectual_humility/introduction_intellectual_humilitty_research.

20 ***more beautiful than we realize—something we remember when we come into, as Wendell Berry described, "the peace of wild things":*** Wendell Berry, "The Peace of Wild Things," *The Selected Poems of Wendell Berry* (Washington, DC: Counterpoint, 1998).

21 ***Latin word for "earth" (and the root word for human and humility) is humus:*** Latin Dictionary, "humus," accessed January 30, 2025. https://www.latin-dictionary.net/.

22 ***"For you are dust," the scriptures say, "and to dust you shall return":*** Genesis 3:18 (NRSV).

23 ***Because it's going through the dirt like everything and everyone else:*** Michael Gungor, "Vapor," meditation, posted March 14, 2014, by The Liturgists, YouTube, https://www.youtube.com/watch?v=3ELxqIES8v8.

24 ***acknowledging that we're made from the earth and will return to the earth:*** "Participating in God by Letting Go of Illusions," Center for Action and Contemplation, posted August 2, 2017, adapted from Richard Rohr, *Simplicity: The Freedom of Letting Go* (New York:

Crossroad Publishing: 2003), https://cac.org/daily-meditations/participating-in-god-by-letting-go-of-illusions-2017-08-02/.

25 ***the nation's highest percentage of coastal erosion:*** City of New Orleans Office of Homeland Security and Emergency Preparedness, "Coastal Erosion," City of New Orleans Housing Mitigation Plan, accessed January 30, 2025, https://ready.nola.gov/hazard-mitigation/hazards/coastal-erosion/.

26 ***"Curiosity is a willingness to withhold drawing conclusions":*** *Igniting Imagination*, podcast, "Expanding Imagination with Amy Oden," TMF and Wesleyan Investive, December 16, 2021, https://ignitingimagination.org/podcast/expanding-imagination.

Chapter Three: Curiosity Disarms Us

29 ***NAFTA paved the way for US manufacturers to relocate to Mexico and Central America:*** Robert E. Scott, "Heading South: U.S.-Mexico Trade and Job Displacement after NAFTA," Briefing Paper 308, Economic Policy Institute, May 3, 2011, https://www.epi.org/publication/heading_south_u-s-mexico_trade_and_job_displacement_after_nafta1/.

29 ***As a result, 1.3 million farm jobs were lost:*** Kimberly Amadeo, "The Disadvantages of NAFTA," The Balance, Dotdash Meredith, updated February 1, 2021, https://www.thebalancemoney.com/disadvantages-of-nafta-3306273.

29 ***Mexican state of Chiapas exploded into its first of many political uprisings:*** Association for Diplomatic Studies and Training, "Trouble in Chiapas: The Zapatista Revolt," May 13, 2016, https://adst.org/2016/05/trouble-chiapas-zapatista-revolt/.

31 ***a fellow Green Valley Samaritan who would be assisting:*** Global Samaritan Resources, accessed January 30, 2025, https://samaritan-center.org.

32 ***A truly nonviolent approach to social change sees no enemies:*** Oren Jay Sofer, *Your Heart Was Made for This: Finding Courage, Expanding*

Connection, and Claiming Joy in Challenging Times (Boulder: Shambhala Publications, 2023), 7.

33 ***become unprecedentedly violent with their own species amid climate-related downsizing:*** Dacher Keltner, *Awe: The New Science of Everyday Wonder and How It Can Transform Your Life* (New York: Penguin Press, 2023).

36 ***the law is written in the sand, not chiseled in hardened stone:*** Deryn Guest et al., eds., *The Queer Bible Commentary* (London: SCM Press, 2015), 993.

37 ***when things become really difficult, urgent, and critical that we should think and act with nonviolence:*** Mark Kurlansky, *Nonviolence: The History of a Dangerous Idea* (New York: Modern Library, 2006), 9.

38 ***assuming that the evil to be overcome is clear-cut, definite, and irreversible:*** Thomas Merton, ed. *Gandhi on Non-Violence: Selected Texts from Mohandas K. Gandhi's Non-Violence in Peace and War* (New York: New Directions, 1965), 27.

39 ***drug dealers who were Rosie's enemy became her friends:*** Johannes Myors, "Allendale Garden of Hope and Love," accessed January 30, 2025, https://allendalegardenofhopeandlove.weebly.com/.

40 ***Guys have underestimated me my entire life. And for years, I never understood why:*** *Ted Lasso*, season 1, episode 8, "The Diamond Dogs," written by Jason Sudeikis et al., directed by Declan Lowney, aired August 21, 2020 on Apple+.

Chapter Four: Curiosity Slows Us Down

44 ***When everything feels heavy, I've learned to travel light:*** Sleeping At Last (Ryan O'Neal), "Atlas: Seven," copyright Asterisk B-612, released as a single on October 12, 2018.

49 ***brain is encoding new memories when you have a novel experience, not mundane experiences:*** The Humane Space, Bites of Curiosity (blog), "The Perception of Time: Part II," July 14, 2024, https://www.thehumane.space/blog-posts/the-perception-of-time-part-ii.

52 ***giving your attention to the new and unfamiliar leads to an expansion in our perception of time:*** Lawton Ursrey, "Curiosity: The One Superpower We Don't Use Enough and How to Use It," *Forbes*, June 20, 2014, https://www.forbes.com/sites/lawtonursrey/2014/06/20/curiosity-the-one-superpower-we-dont-use-enough-and-how-to-use-it/.

53 ***take up "male space, receiving a theological education that authorizes her leadership":*** Deryn Guest et al., eds., *The Queer Bible Commentary* (London: SCM Press, 2006), 955.

54 ***is actually a diagnosable code according to the ICD 10:*** Adam Stacoviak and Mireille Reese, hosts, *Brain Science: Neuroscience, Behavior*, podcast, "Your Brain on Burnout," Changelog Media, December 20, 2022, https://changelog.com/brainscience/33.

55 ***chronic workplace stress that has not been successfully managed:*** World Health Organization, "Burn-out an 'Occupational Phenomenon': International Classification of Diseases," May 28, 2019, https://www.who.int/news/item/28-05-2019-burn-out-an-occupational-phenomenon-international-classification-of-diseases.

55 ***with upwards of 44 percent of individuals experiencing workplace burnout:*** Matt Gonzales, "Here's How Bad Burnout Has Become at Work," Society for Human Resource Management, April 30, 2024, https://www.shrm.org/topics-tools/news/inclusion-diversity/burnout-shrm-research-2024.

55 ***millennials now being called "the burnout generation":*** Anne Helen Petersen, *Can't Even: How Millennials Became the Burnout Generation* (Boston: Houghton Mifflin Harcourt, 2020).

55 ***"five-alarm fire" level, with a 400 percent increase since 2015:*** Western North Carolina Conference of The United Methodist Church, "5 Shocking Realities About the Real State of Pastor Burnout," April 12, 2023, https://www.wnccumc.org/resourcedetail/5-shocking-realities-about-the-real-state-of-pastor-burnout-17392915.

56 ***adopted as the reflexive attitude during each daily interaction, a workday would be infused with enthusiasm:*** Louise Caldwell, "Curiosity as an Antidote to Burnout," OMT Global, accessed January 30, 2025, https://omtglobal.com/curiosity-as-an-antidote-to-burnout/.

58 ***Truly be here, to watch the ones I love bloom:*** Sleeping At Last (Ryan O'Neal), "Atlas: Seven."

Chapter Five: Curiosity Tunes Us In for Transformation

61 ***"Curiosity killed the cat" is a popular (and persistent) idiom:*** Gary Martin, "Curiosity Killed the Cat," Phrase Finder, accessed January 30, 2025, https://www.phrases.org.uk/meanings/curiosity-killed-the-cat.html.

61 ***St. Augustine of Hippo went as far as to list curiosity as one of three kinds of temptation:*** *St. Augustine's "Confessions,"* "Summary and Analysis, Book 10: Chapters 26–34," CliffsNotes, accessed January 30, 2025, https://www.cliffsnotes.com/literature/s/st-augustines-confessions/summary-and-analysis/book-10-chapters-2634.

61 ***noting that hell was fashioned for the inquisitive:*** *St. Augustine's "Confessions,"* trans. Henry Chadwick (Oxford: Oxford University Press, 1991).

63 ***"5 Whys" (a problem-solving tool created by Sakichi Toyoda:*** "Learn About Quality," American Society of Quality, accessed April 28, 2025, https://asq.org/quality-resources/five-whys?

67 ***self identity, a schema consisting of an organised collection of beliefs and feelings:*** Itai Ivtzan et al., "Mindfulness Meditation and Curiosity: The Contributing Factors to Wellbeing and the Process of Closing the Self-Discrepancy Gap," *International Journal of Wellbeing* 1, no. 3 (2011): 316–327.

Chapter Six: Curiosity Pushes Past Shame

77 ***there is a profound difference between shame and guilt:*** Brené Brown, "Shame vs. Guilt," blog entry on official website of Brené Brown, posted January 15, 2013, https://brenebrown.com/articles/2013/01/15/shame-v-guilt/.

77 ***the curious mindset wonders, "Is there something I am needing right now?":*** Emily Sanders (@emily.sanders.therapy), "It's too much to

carry alone. And we were never meant to." Instagram, November 16, 2024, https://www.instagram.com/emily.sanders.therapy/p/DCcvU0BzRNx/.

81 ***humanity's sin as a result of imperfection not inherent corruption:*** Alfred J. Kolatch, *The Jewish Book of Why* and *The Second Jewish Book of Why*, 2 vols. (New York: Jonathan David Publishers, 2000).

81 ***the journey of Adam and Eve can be interpreted as a coming-of-age story:*** Clare Kemmerer, "Eve, Adam, and Innocence: Eden as a Land of Childhood." Witnessing Medieval Evil: Violence and Sin in Art, Literature, and Politics (blog), UChicago Voices, April 26, 2020, https://voices.uchicago.edu/witnessingmedievalevil/2020/04/26/eve-adam-and-innocence-eden-as-a-land-of-childhood/.

82 ***sees themselves as a bad person, they might not see a way out of their situation:*** Stop It Now! UK & Ireland, "Guilt and Shame," accessed January 30, 2025, https://www.stopitnow.org.uk/self-help-module/guilt-and-shame/.

82 ***Shame has detrimental effects on our physical health, our mental well-being:*** "Shame," *Psychology Today*, accessed January 30, 2025, https://www.psychologytoday.com/us/basics/shame.

83 ***can do to protect ourselves is to develop and practice a sense of Curiosity:*** Dayna W. Sharp, "Curiosity as an Antidote to Anxiety and Shame," blog entry on website of Dayna Sharp, LCSW, updated December 17, 2018, https://www.daynawsharp.com/post/curiosity-as-an-antidote-to-anxiety-and-shame.

Chapter Seven: Curiosity Infuses Meaning

89 ***"Don't just do something; stand there":*** The Quote Investigator, March 14, 2022, https://quoteinvestigator.com/2014/03/22/stand-there/.

89 ***Healthy religion gives us a foundational sense of awe:*** Richard Rohr, "Willing to Be Amazed," Center for Action and Contemplation, December 3, 2023, https://cac.org/daily-meditations/willing-to-be-amazed/.

89 ***poet will muse on "this grasshopper":*** Mary Oliver, "The Summer Day," *New and Selected Poems: Volume One* (Boston: Beacon Press, 1992), 94.

89 ***lyric writer will muse on "rice under black beans":*** "Blessings (reprise)," by Chance the Rapper, track 14 on *Coloring Book* (mixtape), released on Apple Music, 2016.

90 ***painter will muse on paper airplanes:*** Scott Erickson (@scottthe-painter), "May I find freedom in limitation—to fully give myself to what I can do rather than worry about what I cannot," Instagram, February 26, 2024.

90 ***the prophet will muse on ashes:*** Isaiah 61:3 (NRSV).

93 ***arose on that day a great persecution against the church in Jerusalem:*** Acts 8:1 (NRSV).

93 ***site of transformation, where the stranger becomes friend:*** Deryn Guest et al., eds., *The Queer Bible Commentary* (London: SCM Press, 2006).

94 ***stories of great significance in the Bible end with the Spirit of God carrying people away:*** Elton Sherwin, host, "The Baptism of the Ethiopian Eunuch," episode 9 of *The Queer Christian: Navigating Faith, Church, and the Bible*, Apple Podcasts, February 8, 2022, https://affirmingscripture.com/episode/9-the-baptism-of-the-ethiopian-eunuch.

94 ***considered sexually other and socially marginalized:*** Preston Sprinkle, "Eunuchs: Male, Female, or Other?" Theology in the Raw (blog), October 15, 2015, https://theologyintheraw.com/eunuchs-male-female-or-other/.

97 ***meaning in life as a fundamental human need:*** Clay Routledge and Taylor A. FioRito, "Why Meaning in Life Matters for Societal Flourishing," *Frontiers in Psychology* 11 (2021), https://doi.org/10.3389/fpsyg.2020.601899.

Chapter Eight: Curiosity Connects Us

101 ***Great improvisers continually practice empathy and curiosity:*** Jay Gerhart, "Two Easy Improv Games for Healthcare Professionals," Atrium

Health, accessed January 30, 2025, https://cdn.atriumhealth.org/-/media/human-resources/documents/hr/twoeasyimprovgames.pdf.

101 ***"Mother Teresa was once asked in an interview, 'What do you say when you pray?'":*** Shane Claiborne and Jonathan Wilson-Hartgrove, *Becoming the Answer to Our Prayers: Prayer for Ordinary Radicals* (Lisle, IL: InterVarsity Press, 2008), 11.

104 ***only 57 percent of Americans know some of their neighbors:*** Leslie Davis and Kim Parker, "Facts about Neighbors in U.S.," Pew Research Center, August 15, 2019, https://www.pewresearch.org/short-reads/2019/08/15/facts-about-neighbors-in-u-s/.

105 ***benefits of well-connected neighborhoods—including fewer lives lost to traumatic events:*** Erica Pandey, "The Weakening Bonds between Americans and Their Neighbors," Axios, July 28, 2022, https://www.axios.com/2022/07/28/neighborhood-connections-knowing-neighbors-strong-society-americans.

105 ***Greek for "broke/break" here is klaio:*** Abarim Publications' Online Biblical Dictionary, "The Meaning of Klaio," accessed January 30, 2025, https://www.abarim-publications.com/DictionaryG/k/k-l-a-om.html.

105 ***visual of a bursting delta, where the waters of the rushing Mississippi shoot out:*** National Geographic Encyclopedia, "Delta," last updated March 14, 2025, https://education.nationalgeographic.org/resource/delta/.

106 ***Turquoise Tables have become a symbol of hospitality, a safe place to sit down:*** Kristin Schell, The Turquoise Table, accessed January 30, 2025, https://theturquoisetable.com/about/.

107 ***idea of "survival of the fittest" has permeated our science, history, and sociological conversations:*** Darwin Correspondence Project, "Survival of the Fittest," University of Cambridge, accessed January 30, 2025, https://www.darwinproject.ac.uk/commentary/survival-fittest.

111 ***have two or three marriages in this life. And if we're lucky, they're with the same person:*** Esther Perel (@esterperel), "In the west today most

people are going to have two or three marriages . . .," Facebook, April 21, 2013, https://www.facebook.com/esther.perel.

113 ***timeless and quirky movie* When Harry Met Sally:** *When Harry Met Sally*, directed by Rob Reiner, produced by Castle Rock Entertainment and Nelson Entertainment, released July 21, 1989.

114 ***Marriage is not the end of romance, it is the beginning:*** Esther Perel, *Mating in Captivity: Unlocking Erotic Intelligence* (New York: Harper, 2007), 242.

Chapter Nine: Curiosity Catalyzes Creativity

125 ***Johannes Gutenberg would go on to invent the movable-type printing press:*** Biography.com, "Johannes Gutenberg," November 28, 2023, https://www.biography.com/inventors/a45975535/johannes-gutenberg.

126 ***partner in what would later be known as the Great Reformation as the wife to Martin Luther:*** Joshua J. Mark, "Katharina von Bora," World History Encyclopedia, December 17, 2021, https://www.worldhistory.org/Katharina_von_Bora/.

126 ***theory of scientific revolutions is referenced frequently to describe and understand shifts like Luther's revolution:*** Thomas S. Kuhn, *The Structure of Scientific Revolutions* (Chicago: University of Chicago Press, 1962).

126 ***anomaly arises "when a puzzle, considered as important or essential in some way, cannot be solved":*** David Blitz, "Thomas Kuhn and Paradigm Shifts," Readings on History and Philosophy of Science, Central Connecticut State University, accessed January 30, 2025, https://bertie.ccsu.edu/naturesci/Evolution/Unit10Background/Kuhn.html.

127 ***a predictable cultural and religious cycle stretching back in various places over millennia:*** Daniel Cash, "Something Like a 500-Year Rummage Sale," blog entry on website of Daniel Cash, posted May 6, 2019, https://danielcash.org/2019/05/06/something-like-a-500-year-rummage-sale/.

129 ***To be the kind of curious creators who "make prototypes, not presentations":*** Matt Rawle and Rachel Billups, hosts, *In the Sandbox*, podcast, Soundcloud.

129 ***a hundred years to shake it all out once more, to find a new normal as humans, as Christians:*** Phyllis Tickle, *The Great Emergence: How Christianity Is Changing and Why* (Grand Rapids: Baker Books, 2008).

Chapter Ten: Curiosity Rewilds Us

144 ***took my son to see the movie* The Wild Robot:** *The Wild Robot*, directed by Chris Sanders, produced by DreamWorks Animation, released September 27, 2024.

146 ***"The unfamiliar road could be the same place you get lost and find yourself":*** "Kiss the Sky," by Maren Morris, track 1 on *The Wild Robot* soundtrack, Back Lot Music, released August 28, 2024.

Chapter Eleven: Curiosity Activates Awe

153 ***which had served as an invitation for curiosity to serve as a midwife:*** Dacher Keltner, *Awe: The New Science of Everyday Wonder and How It Can Transform Your Life* (New York: Penguin Press, 2023), 7.

154 ***"With his passing, I felt aweless":*** Dacher Keltner, *Awe*, xxiv.

154 ***"is the feeling of being in the presence of something vast":*** Dacher Keltner, *Awe*, 7.

155 ***"awe allows us to get outside of ourselves, and integrates us into larger patterns":*** Dacher Keltner, *Awe*, 64.

156 ***God's power isn't in the control of creation or of people, but in being in covenant relationship with them:*** David Roberts, "When God Sleeps Through Storms (Lectionary Reflection on Theodicy for Mark 4:35–41)," Edges of Faith (blog), Patheos, last updated August 29, 2015, https://www.patheos.com/blogs/davidhenson/2015/06/1804/.

161 ***Long lay the world in sin and error pining:*** *O Holy Night (Cantique de Noël)*, lyrics by Placide Cappeau, music by Adolphe Adam, first published in 1843; English translation by John Sullivan Dwight, 1855.

Chapter Twelve: Curiosity Rewrites with Hope

164 ***There aren't as many fireflies as there used to be, scientists say:*** Will County Forest Preserve District, "Five Fun Facts About Bioluminescent Lightening Bugs," July 16, 2021, https://www.reconnectwithnature.org/news-events/the-buzz/lightning-bugs-5-things.